LEGENDARY
OUTLAWS OF THE WEST

LEGENDARY

OUTLAWS

OF THE WEST

Brad Williams

Illustrations by
Paul Blaine Henrie

Henry Z. Walck, Inc.
A Division of
David McKay Company, Inc.
New York

Library of Congress Cataloging in Publication Data

Williams, Brad.
    Legendary outlaws of the West.

    SUMMARY: Biographical sketches of eleven less notorious but notable western outlaws who plundered everything from stagecoaches to airplanes.
    1. Crime and criminals—The West—Juvenile literature. 2. The West—Biography—Juvenile literature. [1. Robbers and outlaws—The West. 2. The West—Biography] I. Title.
F591.W717   364.1'523'0922 [B] [920]   75-43036
ISBN 0-8098-5006-0

Contents

For almost a decade he was the most feared bandit in southern Arizona and northern Mexico. . . . Other than the facts that he raided, pillaged and murdered, nothing is known of him. The newspapers of that era assumed that everyone knew of "Chacón," thus there was no need to write anything about the man other than his latest crime.

Preface

OUTLAWS and the Old West bring together a variety of names. There were Billy the Kid, Frank and Jesse James, Butch Cassidy and the Sundance Kid, the Dalton brothers, and Wyatt Earp. Stories about them and many others have been written down, turned into ballads, and filmed, and because of this, these men are not mentioned in this book.

This is a collection of stories about men who are legendary in the West but whose exploits have not been sung so loudly elsewhere. Nevertheless, they have contributed just as much to the folklore of the West as have their more notorious fellow felons. The careers of some of these legendary bandits have already been lost to history. There is the famous Augustin Chacón, for example, who lived with his band of cutthroats in the Sierra Madre mountains of Mexico in the late 1800s. He raided towns on both sides of the border with impunity. For almost a decade he was the most feared bandit in southern Arizona and northern Mexico. There are many slight references to the dreaded Chacón in the newspapers of the time, but, other than the fact that he raided, pillaged, and murdered, nothing is known of him. The newspapers of that era assumed that everyone knew of Chacón; thus, there was no need to write anything about the man other than his latest crime.

Legend can quickly distort fact. Billy the Kid was not a romantic, dashing hero. Most of his victims were ambushed and shot from behind with a rifle. He was not a handsome man. He had a smooth, beardless face, long hair, sloping shoulders, narrow arms, and wide hips. It is unlikely that anyone mourned his passing when he was trapped and shot by Sheriff Pat Garrett in Fort Sumner, New Mexico. Yet the name of William Bonney, alias Billy the Kid, has become etched into the history of the Old West.

In the early nineteen thirties, a large motion-picture studio in Hollywood was making a film on the Billy-the-Kid legend. The producers found Mrs. John Bowe of New Mexico, an elderly lady who had known Billy the Kid, and hired her as a technical advisor. She was brought to Hollywood, and for two or three days she watched the filming. She then sought out the director. "You've got it all wrong," she said. "You're making a hero out of this boy. He was a psychopathic killer, a very dirty, mean boy whom everyone avoided like the plague."

"Maybe so," the director replied, "but not according to the legend."

Jesse James is a legend. He was not an exceptional bandit. In no manner was he as successful in his chosen field as was Tiburcio Vasquez. His name is known all over the world, however; the only memento to Vasquez are scattered piles of volcanic boulders near Los Angeles, California. The legend of Wyatt Earp as a tough lawman also is well known. Earp was a crook, a bunco artist, a thief, and a panderer, yet his exploits are relatively insignificant when compared to the activities of Sheriff Henry Amos Plummer or Sheriff Burt Alvord.

Plummer and Alvord, Vasquez and Murietta are names of the legendary West that deserve as much attention as those of Earp, Bonney, and James, and their stories are included in this book. As with all legends, there may be points that are not historically accurate. Indeed, as in the story of D. B. Cooper, it is shown how legends can deviate from facts within a few hours after the root of the legend has been planted. There is, however, a root for all of these stories. There was a Black Bart. There were an El Chato, a Tom Bell, and a Black Jack. All of the stories in this book are basically true.

For help provided in preparing this work, the author is grateful to Dick Pace of Virginia City, Montana; Jack Pement and Doug Baker of the Oregon *Journal* in Portland, Oregon; Leverett Richards of the *Oregonian*; Al Watts of the Seattle *Post Intelligence*; Vince Gullette of the Arizona *Republic Gazette*; Bill Robertson of the Southern Pacific Railroad; Bruce Hamby of the Denver *Post* in Denver, Colorado; Sid Smith of Sutter Creek, California; The Montana Historical Society; The Idaho Historical Society; The Historical Department of the Wells Fargo Bank; and the Denver Public Library's History Division, as well as many others who devoted their time and effort to gathering material for this volume.

—BRAD WILLIAMS

LEGENDARY
OUTLAWS OF THE WEST

His appearance alone would unnerve the most stalwart defender.
His nose was half gone and a scar pulled back his
upper lip into a perpetual sneer.

El Chato

HE was known as El Chato, which translates loosely as "pug nose," and he was the first outlaw to form a band of men on horseback to prey on travelers and convoys in what is now the American Southwest. He operated in an area that centuries later was to become the hunting ground for Billy the Kid, and for more than a decade during the mid-1600s he terrorized all who traveled between the garrison outpost of Santa Fe and New Spain.

Indian bands had attacked white settlements and travelers sporadically ever since Francisco Vasquez de Coronado had founded Santa Fe in 1540. The Indians killed, but the items they stole from their victims were colorful bits of cloth and beads and horses. El Chato killed his victims also, but he stole their gold, silver, jewelry, and money. He had little use for most of the loot, but he knew these were things that the Spanish valued, and he plundered them because he hated them.

El Chato's real name was Pedro Neverez, but there was no Spanish blood in his body. The name had been given to him by a Spanish padre when he was baptized in Chimayo. Legend says that his mother was an Apache or a Comanche and that his father was a Pueblo Indian. He apparently was brought up in Chimayo, during a period when the Church in New Mexico was feuding with the garrison governor. The Church's mission was to convert the Indians to Christianity. The governor thought the mission a pointless one, because in his opinion the Indians were subhuman, worthless beings. He kidnapped many of them, sending them to New Spain, where they were sold into slavery. His soldiers raped Indian women. Corn grown by the Indians to carry them through the winter was confiscated by the garrison troops, and when the Indians hid it between the walls of their homes, the soldiers tore down the dwellings. Blankets were torn from sleeping Indians, and they were left naked to shiver and succumb to the cold. The Indians took a dim view of this "Christian" activity on the part of the garrison, and began slipping away from the pueblos and the Church. When Church officials complained, the governor became irate. On one occasion, he fired his pistol at a padre who had scolded him for abusing the Indians. The bullet missed its target, but struck another padre and an Indian. The friar was superficially wounded. The Indian was killed.

The incident took place in Chimayo. The dead Indian was the father of Pedro Neverez, who was then in his mid-teens. When the shooting erupted, Pedro was standing in the center of the pueblo, and he saw his father fall. The boy ran to his father's side and knelt down, then was seized with sudden rage when he saw the smashed face of his father and knew that he was dead. Pedro Neverez picked up a large rock. He threw it with deadly accuracy. It struck the governor on the side of his face, jarring him in the saddle. He cried out, then spotted his assailant. With blood pouring down his face, he spurred his horse and raced toward the boy. At the same time, he unsheathed his sword. Pedro ran. He darted as the horse drew parallel to him. The slashing sword almost missed him. There was a sharp pain on the end of his nose, followed by a warm wetness in his mouth.

Other Indians, crying out in anger, began to throw rocks at the governor and the three soldiers who accompanied him. The padre disappeared. More Indians began running in from the outskirts of the pueblo. The governor suddenly realized that he had precipitated a riot. He called out to his bodyguard, and fled Chimayo in a hail of rocks and stones.

Pedro Neverez's wound was treated by some of the Indian women in the pueblo. The sword had cut off almost half his nose, and one of the sympathic nurses who was washing his body referred to him softly as *"El Chato."* The name was to remain with him for the rest of his life.

The Indians well realized the danger El Chato faced if he remained in the pueblo. Shortly before the following dawn, El Chato was placed in a litter and carried to a sanctuary in the nearby Sangre de Cristo Mountains. The soldiers arrived in Chimayo two or three days later. It was a large detachment, and its members searched the pueblo carefully, looking for the wounded lad who had assaulted the governor. The Indians told the soldiers that the assailant was a stranger to their pueblo, that he had been passing through, and that he was believed to be a member of the Santo Domingo pueblo. They also told the soldiers that the wound had been slight and that the boy had fled the pueblo moments after the governor had departed. The soldiers searched the area around Chimayo thoroughly before they left.

El Chato knew that they would return and that he was branded. None of the pueblos around Santa Fe would be safe, for the soldiers constantly would appear. His only choice was to go far away.

He followed the Rio Grande south, past Fray Cristobal to Mesilla, and eventually arrived in Paseo del Norte (the area that is now known as El Paso). He remained there for three or four years, but little is known about how he spent his time. It can be presumed, however, that it was there that he recruited the members of his band and made the contacts for an intelligence operation that was to serve him so well for more than a decade.

As a base for his operations, he chose Los Organos Mountains, an isolated wilderness that was shunned even by the Indians. El Chato got to know those remote and hostile mountains well. They provided him with a refuge for more than a decade. The mountain range split the two most heavily traveled routes between Santa Fe and Paseo del Norte. One was El Camino Real, which followed the Rio Grande. The other was the more dangerous Jornada del Muerto, the "Journey of Death." This latter route had won its gruesome title because of the untold numbers of travelers who perished on it. During the summer months, temperatures along this desert trail sometimes reached 120 degrees, and the distance was great between water holes. Still, it was widely used, because it shortened the distance between Paseo del Norte and Santa Fe by approximately fifty miles. It went north in a straight line from what is now Las Cruces for a distance of little more than one hundred miles. El Camino Real bowed considerably to the west, but its temperatures were more hospitable to the traveler.

When El Chato first began his operations, blame for them was placed on marauding Apaches. The first victims are believed to have been the drivers of a small wagon train carrying supplies to Mesilla. The six teamsters in the small convoy were found with their throats cut. The value of the loot was unknown, as the wagons had been burned and the horses stolen.

A short time later, another small caravan was raided on the Jornada del Muerto. In this caravan, on horseback, was a royal notary from Mexico City who had joined the group in Paseo del Norte. He was the first to see the bandits swoop out of a narrow canyon and race toward the convoy. The notary sounded the alarm, and the teamsters unsheathed their rifles. The bandits rode right through the convoy, frightening the horses and causing them to bolt. Despite the gunfire, no one was hurt in this first assault. As the bandits turned, the notary caught a glimpse of their leader. His appearance alone would unnerve the most stalwart defender. His nose was half gone, and a scar pulled his upper lip back into a perpetual sneer. Long black hair hung in a braid down the middle of his back. As the notary stared, the bandit raised his pistol and fired. The notary heard the bullet whistle past him and lodge in one of the wagons behind him. The notary waited no longer. Touching his spurs to his horse's flanks, he raced back toward Paseo del Norte. No more shots were fired in his direction. He glanced back over his shoulder. El Chato was leading his men into the caravan again, and again there was the sound of gunfire.

A detachment of soldiers from Paseo del Norte accompanied the royal notary back to the ambush site. The scene was a repetition of the previous attack. The wagons had been burned. The drivers had been slaughtered: two dead of gunshot wounds, the others with their throats slashed. There was no evidence of the cargo's having been burned, however, and once again the horses had been taken. The detachment followed the trail into the canyon. There they either lost it or were reluctant to proceed into territory where they easily could be ambushed.

The military in El Paso made note of the description of the half-nose bandit given by the royal notary. Over the next few months, several patrols were sent out from Paseo del Norte to search for El Chato, but there was no sight of him. There is a strong probability that during this time El Chato was back in the city. He had built an extraordinary spy network in Paseo del Norte, and it was necessary to keep the spies in funds. Some of the loot from the two raids began to turn up in the city. A paint horse with distinctive markings was found and identified as one of the horses taken in the ambush. The owner, however, was a substantial citizen, and had a bill of sale from a man passing through. The seller could not be located.

A courier en route to Santa Fe from Mexico City rested for a few days in Paseo del Norte. Shortly after he resumed his journey, he vanished. His horse also appeared in Paseo del Norte. Again, the new owner had a bill of sale, and the seller was traveling to Durango. No trace was ever found of the courier or of the dispatches which he had carried. At the time, his disappearance was not attributed to El Chato. The bandit had not been seen for several months, and the military had assumed that the man with half a nose was a wandering Apache, and that he and his band had drifted on.

The semiannual supply caravan for the garrison at Santa Fe arrived in Paseo del Norte from Mexico City. It was a large convoy. It carried provisions for the troops and money with which to operate the garrison, and was escorting travelers making the hazardous journey to the northern outpost of New Spain. The caravan rested for two days in Paseo del Norte, then headed for Santa Fe. Because there were several women making the trip, the convoy moved along El Camino Real. A half day's journey out of Las Cruces was as far as the convoy went. The bandits swarmed out of the canyons of Los Organos. Ignoring the gunfire from the four soldiers guarding the caravan, the bandits galloped through the center, slashing harnesses. Two teamsters were decapitated. El Chato was in the middle of the melee, and, according to survivors, he personally killed the four soldiers. None of the bandits sustained injury.

Among the women in the convoy was Doña Beatrice Ortega de Padilla. When the bandits struck, she climbed down from the wagon in which she was riding and then, paralyzed by fear, pressed her back rigidly against one of the wagon wheels, screaming silently. El Chato pulled his horse to an abrupt stop in front of her. For a long moment he stared at the young woman; then, slowly, he pointed his sword at her. Its shaft was red with blood. She wore a white rebozo, fastened over her breasts by a diamond brooch, and the tip of the sword caught the rebozo and tore at it impatiently, until he had pulled it open. El Chato held the rebozo, speared on the tip of his sword, aloft like a flag. It was a gesture of victory, and some of the bandits, seeing it wave in the wind, cheered. Then El Chato lowered his sword, tore the diamond brooch from the cloth, and threw the rebozo to the ground. With his sword, he pointed to the pearl necklace she wore, and she raised her hands to the back of her neck, unclasped it, and handed it to him. El Chato dropped the necklace and the brooch into his saddlebag, hesitated for a moment, then dismounted. On the ground, he appeared to be a much smaller man. Still carrying his sword, he leaped into the wagon, and after a short search he emerged carrying Doña Beatrice's jewelry box. It contained a fortune in gems, diamond pendants, earrings, pins, even a gold cross with diamonds set in it. Doña Beatrice now found her voice. She screamed loudly, and threw herself on the bandit, striking at him with her fists. El Chato merely pushed her away. When she came at him again, he threw her to the ground, then jumped back onto his horse.

The horses that had been cut loose from the wagons were now marshaled to serve as pack animals. The bandits unloaded the wagons, taking arms and ammunition and supplies and loading them onto the horses. They ignored the survivors, who huddled in the heat some distance from the wagons. None of them had been injured, and the fatalities were limited to the two teamsters and four soldiers. The slings on the pack horses were improvised, and it took a considerable amount of time to load them. Eventually, however, El Chato had the animals packed so that they could not carry another pound. A torch was put to the wagons.

Doña Beatrice cried out as the flames shot up from the convoy. El Chato heard her cry, and slowly rode over to where she stood with other survivors.

"What do you plan to do with us?" Doña Beatrice demanded.

El Chato suddenly began to laugh. The other bandits joined in his merriment. "It was a shrieking of madmen," Doña Beatrice wrote to her father later, describing the raid. "I could hear their foul laughter long after they had disappeared from view."

El Chato had left alive thirty-six men and seven women. Three men died in the arduous trek back to what is now Las Cruces. The survivors had no food, but they did have plenty of water from the Rio Grande. Late the following afternoon, they stumbled into Las Cruces. One of the men rode a borrowed mule back to Paseo del Norte while the rest of the survivors rested and ate food provided by friendly Indians.

The military in Paseo del Norte was enraged. Doña Beatrice, the daughter of a prominent general in Mexico City, only recently married, was en route to join her husband in Santa Fe. In interrogating the survivors some days later, the military learned that, aside from the supply wagons, only the wagon carrying Doña Beatrice had been searched by El Chato. She traveled with one maid. There were five other women in the convoy, but the wagons in which they traveled had not been touched.

Military officials concluded from this that El Chato had been given advance notice that the rich Dona Beatrice would be traveling in the convoy, probably while the caravan had waited in Paseo del Norte for four days. Military investigators focused their attention on a man named Miguel Hernandez, who had left the city for the north a day after the convoy had arrived, and returned shortly before the survivors arrived in Las Cruces. Hernandez was picked up for questioning. The interrogation was so intense that he failed to survive it.

A large military force was put together and sent out to the scene of the ambush. The remains of the victims were buried near the charred remnants of the wagons. The expedition followed the trail of the outlaws into the mountains, but the soldiers would not stay in the mountains overnight, preferring to camp in the comparative safety of the desert floor, where sentries could sound the alarm in case of attack. They spent more than three weeks on this in-and-out search mission before reaching the conclusion that El Chato no longer was in the area. Upon their return to Paseo del Norte, they discovered that while they had been on the western side of the mountain range, El Chato had swooped down on a small wagon train traveling down the Jornado del Muerto on the eastern side.

The Indians in the pueblo near Santa Fe were becoming more restless. Although another half century would pass before they revolted successfully, Indian attacks on Spanish settlers were not uncommon. At the same time, the feud between the Church and the military continued. Church officials in Santa Fe decided to remove some of their more valuable artifacts from the outlying pueblo to the comparative safety of the provincial capital. They used friendly Indians to gather up the valuables of the Church from communities as far away as Taos and bring them to Santa Fe.

This act on behalf of the Church infuriated the governor, who saw it as a political ploy by the Church to bring pressure on him from Mexico City. He dispatched a courier to Mexico City to carry his complaint over this political activity by the Church to his superiors. He requested that the military in Mexico City ask the Church hierarchy to order the padres to return the artifacts to the various communities around Santa Fe. The governor's actions were reported to the bishop in Santa Fe, who responded by ordering the artifacts returned to Mexico City. They were packed into two wagons, which were marked boldly by crosses. The governor ordered the wagons not to leave the area. The Church, however, sent the wagons, accompanied by two men, on their way south, and the governor did not dare interfere.

This all took place in the late spring, when the temperatures along the Jornada del Muerto were moderate. The Church wagons, protected by the sign of the cross, chose to travel over the Jornada del Muerto. They were intercepted by El Chato near his usual ambush site. This time, El Chato had brought his own pack horses. He and his men removed the Church treasures from the wagons, then turned them around and told the drivers to return to Santa Fe. "Convey my thanks to the padres," he said.

Reports vary over the value of the treasure, but all agree that the theft enraged the Church, the governor, and the military. This time, a search mission was sent out from Santa Fe to run down the nefarious El Chato, but the trail was very cold by the time the detachment arrived at the foot of Los Organos Mountains. The search went on for three weeks without success, although this time the soldiers swept the mountain passes, canyons, and mesas without retreating to the desert floor to spend the night.

Word of the theft of the invaluable icons arrived in the capital of New Spain some time after receipt of the governor's dispatch protesting their removal. The archbishop and the viceroy decided that the best answer to the dispute was to transfer the governor and his top aides back to Spain, along with the top members of the Church hierarchy. A few weeks later, their replacements arrived in Santa Fe, slipping past Los Organos Mountains without attracting so much as a nod from El Chato.

The new prelate immediately found it difficult to sell Christianity without relics and icons. His superiors in Mexico City agreed. A collection was made of gold and silver chalices, crosses, and other religious paraphernalia. It was assembled in Durango, placed in three wagons on which the cross once again was conspicuously painted, and then sent to Paseo del Norte under the guard of twenty-four soldiers from the Durango garrison.

At about the time the convoy left Durango, El Chato struck a three-wagon caravan, operated by a wealthy merchant from Mexico City named Jorge Chavez, headed for Sante Fe. Six members of the Chavez caravan were killed on the Jornada del Muerto. Four others, including Chavez, managed to get back to Paseo del Norte, where the merchant informed the military that his attacker had only half a nose. There is no evidence of any response by the military.

The caravan from Durango arrived in Paseo del Norte, and, as was the custom, its members rested there for two days. One of El Chato's spies slipped away from the city. After he departed, another pack train arrived in Paseo del Norte. This was a small group, accompanied by Augustinian monks who had started out from Acolman, near Mexico City, for Taos, where they planned to open a mission. These monks also carried an assortment of gold crosses, baptismal urns, chandeliers, and chalices, and an altar cloth woven with gold thread, as well as a large amount of gold coin. The monks had heard of El Chato, and were delighted when their request to join the heavily armed caravan from Durango was granted. The caravan chose the Jornada del Muerto route.

El Chato came out of the same canyon he had used in other raids on the Jornada del Muerto. His band now was larger then it had ever been before. Some guessed it contained about sixty men, others one hundred. It is incredible that the soldiers were not more alert. The band was upon them before they could get together in some formation of defense. The pattern was the same. The bandits swept through the convoy, cutting the traces of the mules and horses. In less than five minutes, every soldier was dead. So were two of the bandits and one of the Augustinian monks. The treasure was packed on the mules. One of the monks reported that the band had appeared and disappeared in less than fifteen minutes.

The military responded in character to this latest outrage, virtually stripping the garrison at Paseo del Norte of troops and joining that force with an equally large detachment sent down from Santa Fe. For several weeks soldiers combed the mountains, then turned to the desert, searching towns such as Mesilla and rooting through small Indian pueblos. All the persons they interrogated had heard of El Chato, but none admitted ever having seen him. There was no sign of El Chato. The expedition eventually returned to its base. Caravans had piled up in Paseo del Norte and in Santa Fe, the shippers and teamsters reluctant to make the journey past Los Organos Mountains. El Chato had effectively laid siege to Santa Fe.

A gigantic freight train was formed in Paseo del Norte, accompanied by more than one hundred fifty soldiers. The trip was a success. There was no sign of El Chato. A similar guard successfully brought a large caravan back from Santa Fe. During the ensuing year, the freight trains were combined and escorted by guards, at least one hundred fifty strong, and there still was no sign of El Chato. The military brass in Mexico City began to complain of the expense. Orders went out to the garrisons in Paseo del Norte and Santa Fe to stop such activity. The freighters thought El Chato probably had long since fled the area, and did not complain when the guards were removed. A small freight team set out for the north. It was ambushed by El Chato on El Camino Real. One person escaped to tell the military that the leader of the bandit gang had only half a nose.

In Santa Fe, the new prelate began to wonder if the military or some parts of it might not be in collusion with El Chato. It seemed very strange that a bandit could operate so successfully for such a long period of time—unless, of course, he did have spies working for him in both the Santa Fe and Paseo del Norte garrisons. There was something else that also struck him as strange: None of the valuables stolen from the Church trains had turned up. Usually stolen property had a way of showing up somewhere, especially in those sparsely populated areas. The idea of a conspiracy grew stronger as El Chato once again began to pick off freight convoys. Some got through, but invariably shipments of value seemed to wind up in El Chato's possession.

Finally, the prelate sent a message with a summary of his suspicions to his counterpart in Durango. Durango was far enough away from Paseo del Norte so that soldiers on one garrison had little if any contact with soldiers at the other. Also, the Durango prelate was on very friendly terms with the commanding officer of the Durango garrison. The two men came up with a plan.

Secretly they put together an undercover operation. Some thirty soldiers were dressed as monks. A pack train was assembled and, accompanied by the pseudo monks, headed north.

At Paseo del Norte, the pseudo monks rested for the customary two days. Their leader reported to the local garrison, requesting armed guards to accompany them for the portion of the trip past Los Organos, as they were carrying an extremely valuable cargo of religous objects to the Taos mission. The request was turned down, and the warning was given that the monks traveled at their own risk. The leader was asked which route he planned to take.

"Jornada del Muerto. It's shorter."

It was about noon when the slow-moving pack train reached the charred remnants of a wagon train. Almost as if on cue, some horsemen emerged from a nearby canyon, moving at a slow gallop toward the pack train. There were nine men on horseback and twenty-five pseudo monks on foot. The bandits approached the pack train carelessly. The man in front had but half a nose, and he carried an unsheathed sword. He gestured toward one of the pseudo monks with his sword, then bent down to take the reins of the lead pack mule. The pseudo monk raised his robe, quickly took out his pistol, and shot El Chato's horse. At the same time, the other "monks" pulled out their pistols and shot at the other bandits. Seven of the nine outlaws fell from their saddles, mortally wounded. One other was wounded, but not seriously, and the mutilated but unharmed El Chato slowly raised his hands.

The elated "monks" tied El Chato onto one of the pack mules and, after a halfhearted and futile attempt to capture the bandits' riderless mounts, turned back to Paseo del Norte. The dead bandits were left on the sand. The wounded bandit successfully feigned death and was also left behind.

El Chato was thrown into the jail at Paseo del Norte. The commander of the garrison there was angry because he had not been let in on the ruse, and the leader of the pseudo monks feared that El Chato would be allowed to escape. He conveyed his fears to the ranking prelate in the city. Three priests were immediately delegated to watch over the prisoner in eight-hour shifts in case he wished to confess his sins. A messenger was sent to Mexico City to inform authorities there of the capture of the notorious bandit, but there was no immediate reply. El Chato said nothing.

The other bandit who had survived the trap managed to find his horse and ride into the community of Robledo, where a girlfriend nursed him. Within approximately three weeks, he had healed sufficiently to venture out into the town. There he had the misfortune to literally bump into one of El Chato's victims, who recognized him. He was immediately arrested, and on the following day was brought to trial in Robledo. The trial was brief. The accused was found guilty and sentenced to be hanged. When the bandit asked for absolution, a local priest was summoned and sent to his cell.

The bandit was most talkative. He told the priest where El Chato had kept his headquarters in Los Organos Mountains and described a nearby cave where most of the booty was stored. After the bandit was hanged, the priest wrote a letter to the Alcoman Monastary passing on the information given him by the outlaw.

The letter, which is still in existence, describes the cave as a natural one facing south near the top of a hill in Soledad Canyon. A cross cut into the rock crested the cave's entrance, which was partially hidden by a juniper tree. Three medium-sized peaks were to the east of the cave. To the north was a dripping spring. The distance from the top of the hill, where one could look down on the Jornada del Muerto for miles, to the entrance of the cave was two hundred fifty paces. The interior of the cave was divided into two parts, which were connected by a short tunnel. It was in this second cave that El Chato had stored most of his loot. He had had no use for it. It had been taken only because it was valued so highly by the white invaders. The currency and coins taken, and the proceeds received from the sale of valuables, had been used to pay off the spies and informers in Paseo del Norte. According to the bandit, El Chato had kept a record of the number of persons he had killed: one hundred twenty-seven deaths for half a nose.

Approximately one month after the hanging in Robledo, word arrived in Paseo del Norte to send El Chato to Mexico City. Any records of what happened to El Chato after he was taken from Paseo del Norte have disappeared. It is generally believed that he was tried in the capital of New Spain and hanged.

The letter written by the priest who heard the Robledo confession came to light quite by accident. In 1877, a band of marauding Apaches attacked the mission in Dona Ana. After putting the church to the torch, they fled, carrying with them some boxes that they apparently thought held valuables. There was nothing but papers in the boxes, however, and the Indians threw these to the winds on the mesa. The letter was among those papers that were salvaged.

El Chato was the first of the Western bandits to form a gang of desperados and conduct his raids in a paramilitary manner. He established a pattern that was followed principally by Mexican outlaws for the next two centuries, but no subsequent bandit chieftain ever had as efficient a system of spies and informants as did the bandit with half a nose.

Reports still are made of the sudden appearance of a headless horseman wrapped in a black serape. . . .

"I am Joaquin," the apparition wails, "and I want my head."

Joaquin Murietta

ON a beach near La Paz, in a cantina near Guadalajara, or on a ranch in New Mexico—wherever the mariachis gather—they will sing eventually the ballad of Joaquin Murietta. In some ways, the ballad parallels the tale of "The Headless Horseman" made famous by Washington Irving. In many parts of the West and Mexico, he is a Latin bogeyman, and impatient Mexican mothers still hush their querulous children most effectively with the warning that Joaquin Murietta will get them if they don't watch out.

In California—from Cantua Arroya, near Coalinga, to Murphy's Diggings, in the Mother Lode country—reports still are made of the sudden appearance of a headless horseman wrapped in a black serape. "I am Joaquin," the apparition wails, "and I want my head." Sometimes the apparition is not seen, but his forlorn cry is heard throughout the passes of the Coast Range where the infamous outlaw roamed.

For years, a head claimed to have been Murietta's traveled through California immersed in a bottle of brine. It later became a prized attraction in a Barbary Coast saloon in San Francisco. When that city was destroyed by earthquake and fire in 1906, the controversial head disappeared forever. There is strong evidence, however, that the briny head never was attached to the shoulders of the notorious outlaw and that its appearance was part of a carefully planned retirement program for the bloodiest and most ruthless bandit that ever roamed the West.

Billy the Kid, the highly publicized, slope-shouldered, wide-hipped outlaw of the Southwest, killed twenty-one persons before he was slain at the age of twenty-one. Murietta reigned over California for about three years longer than Billy, and at about the same time, yet the most conservative estimate of the number of his victims is in excess of three hundred. There are some who have glamorized him as the Robin Hood of his time, stealing from the rich and giving to the poor. However, his only charitable impulse that can be documented is an occasion when he spared the life of a robbery victim who had saved Murietta's life a few years earlier. His plunder was astronomical, and much of it was shipped to Old Mexico as another contribution to his retirement program.

Joaquin Murietta came to California from his native Sonora in Mexico about a year before the famous Gold Stampede of 1849. His departure from home was abrupt, and designed to elude the wrath of Don José Gonzales, who was planning to marry the girl Joaquin loved.

Murietta lived in the Real de Bayareca between Arispe and Hermosillo, a lush and fertile Sonora valley. In the same valley lived the beautiful Rosita Carmel Feliz. Both Rosita and Joaquin were educated together in the same convent school, attended the same masses in the old plaza church, and danced together at the fandango dances. When she was sixteen and Joaquin eighteen, they fell in love.

In the same valley lived Don José Gonzales, a gentleman who was very old and very rich. Once he had been prominent at the court of the first Mexican emperor, Augustine Iturbide. His Sonora hacienda was measured in square kilometers instead of acres. He owned five thousand head of cattle. What Don José wanted, he bought, and when he saw Rosita leaving mass one day, he decided that she should replace the wife he had buried a few months earlier.

Don José opened negotiations with Ramon Feliz, the impoverished father of Rosita. Feliz, apparently envisioning a sharp upturn in his financial status, quickly agreed to the publishing of the banns. However, they were the only persons who agreed to the match. Rosita's brother, Reyes Feliz, was irate. Equally upset were Joaquin's brothers Claudio and Antonio, as probably would have been an older Murietta brother, Carlos Jesús, had he not left for somewhere in California a few years earlier.

The day the wedding date was announced, Joaquin and Rosita permanently borrowed two of Don José's blooded horses and in the middle of the night fled from the Real de Bayareca. They were married the following morning in Arispe. They continued their flight along the Camino del Diablo, the deadly and bleak trail that crossed the deserts south of Arizona, and eventually reached the city of Los Angeles.

At that time, Joaquin had two talents. He was an expert horseman. For almost a year, he had worked as a groom in the stables of President Lopez de Santa Anna in Mexico City, and there were no horses in that great stable that Joaquin could not handle. He was also extraordinarily adept in the manipulation of cards. In Los Angeles, he worked at two jobs—as a horse trainer and a monte dealer—and in his spare time he roamed through the pueblo looking for his older brother, Carlos Jesús. A few months later, he drifted north with Rosita. He dealt monte in gambling halls at San Juan Bautista and later at San Jose. He opened a store in Stockton, went broke, and then broke horses on a ranch near Mount Diablo. It was here that he learned his brother was in San Francisco.

It was an angry Carlos Jesús that Joaquin found a few weeks later in a gambling hall adjoining the Barbary Coast. Carlos, it seemed, had purchased some land near Hangtown (now known as Placerville), but with the advent of the Gold Rush, the title had somehow become obscured, and the original owner was claiming that the money for the property had never been paid. There was a witness to the transaction, however, a young Mexican named Flores who lived in Hangtown.

Rosita was left at the home of a friend, Manuel Sepulveda, in San Francisco while the two brothers departed by stage for Sacramento. Horses there were scarce and expensive. The Muriettas bought two mules and traveled the rest of the way to Hangtown on the animals. There they discovered that Flores had moved on to Murphy's Diggings, another day and a half's journey. This town was booming. Gold had been discovered in many adjacent areas, and Murphy's Diggings was the gathering point for all the gamblers, prostitutes, con men, merchants, and miners in all of Calaveras County.

The Muriettas found Flores in a hotel tavern, joined him at a table, and explained the reason for the journey. So far as Carlos Jesús was concerned, there was nothing secret about his mission. All that he wanted Flores to do was sign an affidavit, prepared by a San Francisco attorney, that Flores had been a witness to the payment of the money. It is unknown whether Flores signed the papers, but Carlos and Flores did decide to take a look around the town, and Joaquin offered Flores the use of his mule.

A few moments later, Joaquin heard a tremendous uproar in the streets. When he went out to investigate, he discovered his brother and Flores surrounded by some twenty drunken miners. Haranguing Carlos Jesús as a thief was a burly brute, later identified as Bill Lang. It was Lang's contention that the two mules on which Flores and Carlos were riding had been stolen from him, and, as mule theft was equally as serious a crime as horse stealing, it took Lang but a few minutes to whip his companions into a hanging mood. Nooses were quickly slipped around the necks of Carlos Jesús and Flores.

Joaquin, crying out in protest, was seized by the gang, and escaped hanging by the proverbial hair. As his brother and Flores died above him, Joaquin was bound to the base of the tree. His shirt was ripped from his body. The huge Bill Lang seized a bullwhip and lashed it across Joaquin's back thirty-nine times. Each stroke was to leave a permanent scar. Legend says Joaquin did not groan or writhe once under the torture. Only his eyes seemed to move from one person to another in the gang, lingering on each face to burn it on his mind as indelibly as the scars on his back. The men commented on it when they returned to the saloon. Lang was not impressed. "If he comes back to town, we'll hang the son of a bitch," he boasted, and poured himself another drink.

Outside, a young gambler named William Wallace Byrnes drifted over to the tree, freed the lacerated Joaquin, and cut down the bodies of the two lynching victims. The bodies were draped over Byrnes's horse and taken to the outskirts of town, where Joaquin and the young gambler dug shallow graves and buried the two men. When the brief and silent funeral was over, Byrnes took Joaquin to his hotel, where he treated the youth's injured back with soothing ointment. Understandably, this was the start of a long and lasting friendship.

For almost a month, despite Lang's threats, Murietta remained quietly in Murphy's Diggings, savoring his hate for the men who had killed his brother and whetting his appetite on thoughts of the gold that lay in the ground all around him. He staked a small claim in nearby Saw Mill Flat and on it built a small, three-room adobe house with the help of other Mexican miners and his friend Bill Byrnes. When the home was finished, he made a quick trip to San Francisco to pick up Rosita, and brought her back to the only home they were to own. And there, if he had been left alone, Joaquin Murietta probably would have mellowed with age and died, like most of the other miners, in obscurity. But Joaquin Murietta was not left alone.

Abutting his claim was a larger one, worked cooperatively by five Americans who were veterans of the recent Mexican-American War. The five Americans bunked together in a large tent, and they made no secret of their hostility to Murietta and all Mexicans. They began to take water from Joaquin's sluice box, and when he objected, they arrogantly began to trench on his claim. The dispute, fanned by racial bias, reached its peak early one evening when the five miners marched into Murietta's small adobe house. Their spokesman bluntly ordered Joaquin and Rosita to get out and go back to Mexico. The melee started when Joaquin sprang for a bowie knife on the table.

The young Murietta was no match for his five assailants. Thrown to the floor, he was kicked and pummeled. Rosita, screaming hysterically, snatched up the bowie knife and moved to her husband's aid. She was quickly disarmed and held against the wall by one of the miners. The other four systematically kicked Joaquin into unconsciousness.

Some time later, Bill Byrnes came to the cabin. He first noticed the unconscious Murietta, ran to a well for a bucket of water, came back, and revived his friend. Joaquin staggered into the adjoining room. Rosita lay spread-eagled and naked on the bed, her limbs bound to the four posts of the cot with the clothes stripped from her body. Her face was battered beyond recognition. As Joaquin moved toward her, Rosita opened her eyes, saw her husband, then sighed deeply. Her eyes closed, and she trembled slightly before she died.

For a long while, Joaquin said nothing. Then slowly he turned from his teen-aged bride and looked at his companion. His face was as expressionless as a mask. When he spoke, his lips barely moved. "By the blood of Christ, I will kill them all," he said slowly.

The five American miners never went back to their claim. Frontier justice, which would have ignored the beating of Murietta, would not tolerate such a brutal sex crime. Joaquin Murietta buried his bride near his adobe house and the next day disappeared from Saw Mill Flat.

Several months later, some prospectors crossed a lonely gulch in the Stanislaus River area near Columbia and made a grisly discovery. Lying on the ground were the remains of five bodies. The ears had been sliced from each head. One of the prospectors in the party recognized a ring on the finger of one of the victims. It was identical to a ring worn by a miner he had known in Saw Mill Flat, who had worked the claim next to Murietta's.

Murietta, meanwhile, was back in Murphy's Diggings, where he opened up a monte game in a local saloon in a partnership with his old friend Bill Byrnes. Murietta lived with a Yaqui Indian named Joaquin Romero in the nearby village of Los Muertos. If anyone recognized him as the youth who had been lashed so severely some months earlier, they said nothing. By then he spoke fluent English, with no trace of an accent, and was very polite and quite dapper in his dress. Shortly after the monte game was opened, Joaquin Murietta moved away from the home of his Indian friend to share quarters with two new arrivals in Los Muertos. One of the newcomers was Reyes Feliz, the brother of Rosita. The other was Joaquin's younger brother Claudio.

One day shortly after the arrival of Claudio, the burly Bill Lang leaned against the door of his saloon and watched a miner lead a loaded burro into town. A crowd gathered, and Lang stepped into the street, then caught his breath. Strapped on the back of the small pack animal was a dead man found by the miner in the chaparral along the trail to Angel's Camp. Around the neck of the body was a deep red scar, and the ears had been slashed off close to the head. It needed no expert to determine what had happened. The victim had been lassoed, dragged into the brush, and horribly tortured before he died. The sight troubled Bill Lang. The dead man had been a friend of his—in fact, one of the twenty who had helped in hanging Carlos Jesús Murietta.

Within the next month, the bodies of four more men were discovered in thickets throughout the hills. All had been slain in the same fashion as the first. All had been members of the Murietta lynching party.

A short time later, a doctor cantered along the trail from Cucumber Gulch to Murphy's Diggings in the late dusk. Hooves drummed behind him on the trail. The doctor turned in his saddle and gasped. A grim figure dressed in black was overtaking him at a tremendous pace. Over the man's head spun a lariat. Suddenly a full moon slid out from behind a cloud, casting its glow over the terrified doctor and the specter. The figure in black reined his mount abruptly and snapped in his lariat. The doctor wheeled, spurred his animal, and raced for Murphy's Diggings, although there was no pursuit. The moonlight, which undoubtedly had spared his life, had also given the doctor time to recognize the mysterious murderer as the quiet-speaking monte dealer of Murphy's Diggings.

The motive and real identity of the killer were established shortly after the doctor and a few others of the townspeople called on the startled Bill Byrnes, who luckily was able to convince his guests that he knew nothing of the extracurricular activities of his monte partner. A delegation of heavily armed miners rode into Los Muertos, but the small house which Joaquin shared with Claudio and Reyes had been abandoned.

The remaining fifteen members of the lynching party sought safety in flight. In pairs and singly, they fled the mining camp. But they could not escape. Joaquin Murietta toyed with them as would a cat with a crippled bird. The sixth member of the lynching party was slain near Stockton; the seventh, a few days later in far-off Knight's Ferry. Murietta seemed to have an uncanny intelligence system that kept him informed as to the precise whereabouts of his victims.

One potential victim was arrested for a murder in Vallecito and brought to Murphy's Diggings for trial. He escaped, and the following morning his earless remains were found on a trail several miles out of town. Another died in a similar fashion in far-off Aurora, Nevada. Four were slain on the same day on the banks of the Merced River. Of the twenty men in the group that hanged Carlos Jesús Murietta and Flores, only two escaped the vengeance of Joaquin, and both of these died violently. One was hanged before Murietta could reach him. The other was Bill Lang, who was shot down during a brawl.

At twenty-one, Joaquin Murietta's death toll was three ahead of the total number slain by Billy the Kid.

But many of his fellow Mexicans thought of his vendetta as more than one of a personal nature. Murietta had been abused by the Americans, but he was not the only Mexican in California to have been maltreated. Many thousands of Mexicans had poured into California during the Gold Rush, still harboring strong anti-American bias engendered during the Mexican War. The Americans resented the Mexican infiltration of the gold fields. The California State Legislature even passed an act which taxed foreign miners exorbitantly, although the tax was repealed a few months later.

Thus, to many Mexicans, in the early stages of his activities Murietta was a great hero. For a while he was nicknamed El Patrio, "The Patriot," and there are some indications that he considered himself a liberator. The name El Patrio, however, did not stick with him long, because, as his orgy of terror spread, the North Americans struck back at everything Mexican. Numerous Mexican communities were put to the torch and all their inhabitants driven out into the mountains. In one instance, an entire Mexican city was leveled by a vengeful mob because Murietta had hidden within its confines.

The Murietta band started small, with Joaquin as its chief and Claudio and Reyes Feliz as its two generals. At the beginning, the trio would raid an isolated mining camp, slaughter its few inhabitants, then fade back into the hills with stolen gold dust and food. Miners traveling the trails were lassoed from their horses and dragged along the ground until they were dead. Ironically, Joaquin, who was so sensitive to maltreatment of his own people, had an unreasoning hatred toward Orientals. Rare indeed was the Chinese who ever faced Murietta and walked away. He went out of his way to find them, and to him the killing of a Chinese was a sport. More than two hundred of his victims were Orientals.

In its formative period, the gang of bandits ranged over an area bounded on the north by Sutter's Creek and on the south by Jackson and Murphy's Diggings. As its reputation spread, it added to its roster as choice a group of thugs as ever slit a throat. Perhaps the most notorious was a pathological killer named Manuel Garcia, better known as Three-Fingered Jack. Other members of the hard-core center of the horde included Joaquin Valanzuela, a survivor of the notorious Jurata gang of Mexico, Luis Vulvia, Pedro Gonzales, Juan Senate, and Rafael Escobar. When the band reached its peak in size, each of these men commanded a full company of desperados operating simultaneously over a hundred-mile front. If one of the companies became pressed by a posse, it would break apart, only to re-form a few weeks later in a different section of the vast state.

When his revenge for Rosita's death was completed, Joaquin did not brood over his lost love. He went back to Sonora, and returned with another childhood sweetheart, named Clarita Valero, but he tired of her quickly and sent her home. Clarita was replaced briefly by a Dolores Garcia, who in turn was dropped in favor of the beautiful and sophisticated Antonia La Molinera.

There are tales that Joaquin took La Molinera out of San Jose at daggerpoint to one of his mountain hideouts. She apparently approved of this manner of courtship. She became his constant companion, sometimes riding the trails with him, dressed like a man, at other times his only partner in the fandango houses that Murietta enjoyed so thoroughly. Except for Bill Byrnes, she was the only person in California who held the complete trust and affection of the bandit.

There were other women in the band, but none with the arrogance, the beauty, and the intelligence of La Molinera. The sweetheart of Pedro Gonzales was Marquita Vasquez. Less restrictive with their favors were Jesusita Espinosa, a Carmelita, and a Maria Ana Benites. The last was confused with La Molinera on several occasions, but there never was any doubt as to which was Murietta's mistress when the two were seen together.

Murietta surely must have thought himself invincible at the conclusion of his first year of operations. The general public reacted in much the same manner as had the twenty-man mob that lynched Carlos Jesús Murietta. Whenever the Murietta horde was rumored to be in the area, townspeople panicked and fled. By the time someone had organized a posse, the bandits were gone. Incredible as it may

seem, during the first year of operation the Murietta band suffered
no known casualties, yet the murders attributed to it were in excess of
one hundred fifty.

Many of the killings were wanton. A newspaper, the Alta *Californian,* reported an incident in which Murietta rode into San Andreas,
singled out three North Americans on the main street, and shot them
dead. "On Thursday," the paper reported, "Joaquin rode through
San Andreas and shot three Americans as he passed through the
street. Joaquin is a young man and must be one of the best shots with a
revolver in this or. any other country as all these men were shot
through the neck." The newspaper did not bother to mention the
names of the victims.

As the horde grew larger and bolder, towns posted armed
guards around their communities. Stagecoaches refused to operate
unless accompanied by heavily armed patrols. Miners abandoned
their claims. The citizens of many communities in the Mother Lode
country banded together to form a small army that had but one
objective: to trap and hang Murietta.

The bandit gang, in view of this threat, split apart temporarily,
but this time the strategy was not completely successful. Two of the
gang were trapped in Sonora, near Marysville, and shot to death after
they wounded a deputy sheriff. Another was hanged in Mokelume
Hill, and still another in Angels Camp. Murietta apparently regarded
these casualties as a matter of lese majesty. He called the band
together again and struck out at everything. Oddly, most of his rage
was directed toward the Chinese mining camps. He burned down a
sawmill, killing three men too old to join the army, then, believing the
army to be much farther south, attempted a retaliatory raid on
Mokelume Hill. He nearly was ambushed at Chaparral Hill as he
moved toward the town, losing a half dozen of his gang.

The citizens' army trailed Murietta to a mountain community
named Yaqui, composed primarily of Mexicans. This posse was well
over one hundred men, all of them angry and bitter. When they could
not find any sign of the bandit or his followers in the community, and
when no one would tell them where they had gone, the army
destroyed the town. Systematically, it put the torch to every home,
every store, and every building in Yaqui. Every inhabitant was driven
into the hills. Today there are no signs of Yaqui. Even its location is a
matter of disagreement among the old-timers of the Mother Lode
country. On its return to San Andreas, the posse, still in the mood for

destruction, burned out the entire Mexican section of the city, sending hundreds of destitute Mexicans into the hills.

Although cruel, the destruction of these two communities achieved the desired result. The Mexicans now feared the citizens' army more than they feared the wrath of Murietta. No longer did they think of him as El Patrio, because he had become responsible for their own misfortune, and thus, no longer did they hide and feed members of the gang in their homes. It no longer was a status symbol for a Mexican youth to ride with Murietta. The size of the band dwindled rapidly, and Murietta decided to turn his attention elsewhere temporarily. As his headquarters he chose the large city of San Jose, many miles to the east in the fertile Santa Clara Valley.

Inside the city, the gang lived quietly, but the harassment of ranchers and travelers outside the city reached such proportions that it soon was known to all that the bandit Murietta was in the area.

The reaction was predictable. Deputy Sheriff Robert Clark formed a posse of the city's more stalwart citizens and eventually trapped two members of the band near the foothills of the Santa Cruz Mountains. The two captives were brought into San Jose for trial. Among the spectators at the proceedings where the two bandits were sentenced to be hanged was Murietta, his identity apparently known only to the defendants.

The day after the two bandits were executed, Deputy Sheriff Clark was tipped anonymously that still another bandit of Murietta's would be at a fandango dance that night in the San Jose Plaza. As Clark leaned against the wall, listening to the music and watching for his man, a woman suddenly screamed. The music stopped, and the dancers parted to disclose a youthful and handsome Mexican waving a knife in front of a terrified girl whom he had pinned against the wall.

Clark reacted as would any deputy. He disarmed the irate Mexican youth easily, and bustled him off to a justice of the peace who was holding night court for just such occasions.

Clark's captive was friendly and understanding, enough so that the deputy suggested to the court that he be assessed only a small fine of twelve dollars. The court agreed.

"I don't have that much money with me," the defendant said apologetically, "but if the Sheriff will be kind enough to walk with me to my home, I will give him the money there."

Both the court and Clark were agreeable to this suggestion from such a pleasant and inoffensive young man. They left the building and strolled along the dark and narrow streets toward the Santa Clara Mission.

"Incidentally, I have a surprise for you," the Mexican said presently.

The deputy paused and smiled at his companion.

"I am Joaquin Murietta," the man said in the same cavalier manner, "and I have brought you here to kill you."

The dying Clark's body was found a short time later, a hand on the butt of his revolver.

The gang moved back toward the east. From Stockton, the river flows down to San Francisco Bay, navigable even today by oceangoing vessels. At that time, it was the more popular mode of transportation and, with bandits like Murietta roaming the countryside, the safest way to travel to San Francisco.

A few days after Clark died in San Jose, a two-masted schooner cast off from the Stockton Wharf. On board were three sailors and two miners with approximately thirty thousand dollars' worth of gold dust. The river writhed through the land on the first part of its journey to the bay, little more than a slough at that time, with tall bulrushes lining the river bank.

It is unlikely that any on board noticed the small rowboat that glided out from the thick brush along the land and, like a leech, fastened itself to the side of the schooner. Moments later, four men leaped onto the deck. The helmsman was shot instantly. One sailor smashed the skull of one of the bandits with a belaying pin, but he died a moment later when a bullet struck him in the head. Within a few seconds, the miners were slain, as was the remaining sailor. Murietta, Three-Fingered Jack, and Valanzuela slipped back into the stolen rowboat and paddled away with the loot.

When word of the murders reached Stockton, the touch of Murietta was suspected. A five-thousand-dollar reward was posted for his capture, and a twenty-five-man posse was formed to track down the outlaw. The posse was no match for the wily Murietta, who, on about the fourth day of the chase, ambushed it, killing twenty-four of its members. The only man to survive was a Jim Boyce, who, ironically, was the only member who had ever seen Murietta. The slaughter of the posse increased Murietta's unpopularity markedly. There was talk in Stockton of building a two-hundred-fifty-man permanent posse to run him down. The Mother Lode country was still unfriendly, and San Jose was most inhospitable. Once again, the gang was disbanded, and told to drift down to Los Angeles. A rendezvous would be held in nearby San Gabriel.

Murietta, Reyes Feliz, Three-Fingered Jack, and Valanzuela traveled to the City of the Angels with Maria Ana Benites, Marquita Vasquez, Carmelita, and another woman. La Molinera was sent on ahead. It was planned as a nice vacation trip. The only business conducted occurred at Tejon Pass, where Murietta noticed a particularly fine horse and decided to take it along with him.

It was a mistake. The horse belonged to a close friend of Tejon Chief Zapatero's, and he had no intention of letting the animal become the property of a few transients. The night after the horse had been stolen, a band of Tejons surrounded the sleeping Murietta party, disarmed it, and marched it some fifteen miles to a stockade in Zapatero's village. A few Indian braves had accomplished easily what a dozen armed posses had been unable to do in the north. The Murietta party was kept in the stockade for a couple of weeks, then stripped of finery, valuables, and horses, marched to the edge of the Tejon domain, and turned loose. The terrorist outlaw and his companions skulked across the county by night until, on the outskirts of Los Angeles, they reached the home of a hoodlum friend known as Mountain Jim Wilson. There horses, pistols, and clothes were found in the usual manner, and the Murietta group was able to regain some of its usual arrogance.

About a week later, Pedro Gonzales and Juan Cardoza drifted into San Buenaventura in their trek to the southland. In this seacoast town south of Santa Barbara was a Los Angeles deputy sheriff named Harry Love. A former Texas Ranger, Love had come to California in the Gold Rush, gone broke, and become a deputy in Santa Barbara before taking a similar position in Los Angeles. A tough-speaking, ugly, and profane man, Love was quick to jump to conclusions. Earlier, a horse had been stolen from J. A. Carver, and the thief later had shot a tavernkeeper. In San Buenaventura, Love was told that Cardoza, well known as a horse thief, had headed south a couple of hours earlier. Love knew Cardoza, but not Gonzales.

At a tavern a few miles south, Love spotted the horses of the two men, and he paused outside to wait for them to emerge. Cardoza came out first and, seeing Love, bounded around the corner of the building and jumped onto his horse. Gonzales rushed out at the sound of the shooting and was immediately taken prisoner. Love tethered Gonzales to the saddle of his horse and set out for Los Angeles, Gonzales trailing behind. Cardoza, meanwhile, rode at breakneck speed to San Gabriel, where Murietta was waiting. The deputy and his prisoner traveled all night, but the pace necessarily was slow. At dawn, in the Conejo Valley north of Los Angeles, Murietta overtook Love and Gonzales. Love was faced with a difficult decision. He was outnumbered by the bandits and captive, yet after all that work he did not want to lose his prisoner. The answer that occurred to Love seemed reasonable. Turning in his saddle, he shot Gonzales, cut him loose, kicked the stolen horse free, then rode for his life to Los Angeles. Thus, Gonzales became the first in the top command of the Murietta gang to die.

Possibly the death of Gonzales was an omen. Murietta found it much more difficult to operate around Los Angeles. He lived in San Gabriel with La Molinera, Maria Benites, Reyes, and Carmelita, but for some reason the band could not get organized as it had in the north. Part of the trouble Murietta blamed on the vigilantes, who were prone to shoot as unpredictably as any bandit. Two members of his band were shot down for no reason at all.

A deputy sheriff from Santa Barbara, Robert Wilson, heard of the five-thousand-dollar reward for Murietta and learned also that the notorious bandit was hiding somewhere in Los Angeles. He rode south, and in the city he spread the word as to the reason for his visit.

One morning he heard a fracas in front of the Bella Union Hotel, where he was staying, and strolled outside. Two men were flailing away at each other, neither doing much damage. A few dozen peons in sombreros watched the fight curiously. Another Mexican, slouched in his saddle, came down the street, and when he drew abreast of Wilson, he casually reined in his horse. "I hear you are looking for me," he said casually.

Wilson looked up. "Who in the hell are you?"

"Joaquin Murietta."

Wilson reached for his gun, but he was not fast enough. He died, a bullet in his brain, with his gun half out of its holster.

This was the type of murder that excited the vigilantes. In the ensuing sweep, three members of the Murietta band were snared and hanged. Murietta reacted in the same manner as he had in Angels Camp.

One of the most prominent members of the vigilantes in Los Angeles was General Joshua H. Bean, a former mayor of San Diego and a major general in the state militia. On the night of November 21, 1852, General Bean was assassinated by Murietta in San Gabriel as he was returning to his quarters in the old mission building.

The reaction to this murder was greater than anything Murietta had ever experienced. The vigilantes swarmed like locusts over San Gabriel. Murietta and Three-Fingered Jack escaped into the hills. Caught by the vigilantes, however, were Maria Benites and Reyes Feliz, along with numerous others of his followers.

There was a trial. Maria Benites testified that a cobbler named Cipriano Sandoval had killed the general. Reyes Feliz was taken for a citizens' trial to Los Angeles, where it was discovered that he was the brother-in-law of the notorious Murietta and a member of his gang. Also caught in San Gabriel was Benito Lopez, another member of Murietta's band.

The trial did not last long. The Sunday after the death of General Bean, Reyes Feliz, Benito Lopez, and the poor cobbler, Cipriano Sandoval, were hanged along with another murderer at Fort Hill in downtown Los Angeles, to the cheers of a crowd of several hundred men and women who had gathered to witness the executions. Two of the top command were gone.

The bandit, with Three-Fingered Jack and two others, retreated farther from the city, to hide out in Mariposa. Word was sent out for the band to rendezvous there. Luis Vulvia, Juan Senate, and four other members of the gang headed for the rendezvous, but on their way out of the city they paused to rob and kill a wealthy French merchant. A squad of deputies headed by City Marshal Jack Whaling intercepted the bandits midway between Los Angeles and San Gabriel. The bandits escaped after killing Whaling, but almost at once the identity of the killers was known, and they were identified as henchmen of Murietta's. Rewards of fifteen hundred dollars posted for Vulvia and Senate, dead or alive.

The following morning, a bull cart driven by a small boy and accompanied by a well-dressed Mexican horseman pulled up in front of the Los Angeles jail. The horseman called for the sheriff and jailer to come out. He was, the horseman explained, Atanacio Moreno, formerly of Yaqui. The preceding day, he continued, he had been kidnapped by five men; as he had been taken along the highway, he had overpowered and slain the lot. The bodies were under the canvas in the bull cart. Two of the men were identified as Vulvia and Senate. The other three were unknown.

Moreno was an overnight hero with his five corpses. He collected the reward, but his hours of glory did not last long. When he tried to sell some of the merchandise stolen from the murdered Frenchman to a local pawnbroker, he was arrested. Word was passed to the authorities that he had been a close companion of Senate's and Vulvia's in many of the city's dives. When questioned about this, Moreno admitted that he had indeed been a member of the Murietta band, but said he had received a message from God to mend his ways and that he had interpreted this as a heavenly directive to do away with his evil comrades. Apparently, the court accepted this explanation as a reasonable one. He was tried only for the theft of the Frenchman's valuables, found guilty, and sentenced to four years in prison. On his release, he disappeared and presumably returned to Mexico.

On the same day that Moreno was found guilty of his minor offense, Mountain Jim and Valanzuela were trapped by sheriff's deputies in a San Diego tavern. Valanzuela shot his way out, but Mountain Jim was captured and, within a period of a half-hour, was tried, found guilty, and hanged. Valanzuela successfully worked his way back to Los Angeles, puzzled as to how the posse had traced him to that particular tavern in San Diego. Both he and Mountain Jim had been completely unknown in that border city. The only reason for his being in the tavern had been to pick up possible orders from Murietta.

In Los Angeles, Valanzuela went to the brothel where Carmelita was employed temporarily, and it was from her that he learned of the perfidy of Maria Benites. In return for her information, the authorities had gratefully released her from custody. Carmelita had no idea where she had gone, but Valanzuela had solved the mystery as to how he had been trapped in San Diego. From Carmelita, he also learned the whereabouts of Murietta.

A short time later, Valanzuela appeared at Joaquin's hideout in Mariposa, where he solved the other mystery—what had happened to Maria Benites. She had been bedding with the notorious bandit while he waited for his scattered band to reach Mariposa. It would be hard to guess who was the most surprised: Valanzuela, at finding her there; Maria, at seeing Valanzuela alive; or Murietta, on learning that his current mistress was surely a sheriff's agent. The bandit, however, was not gallant; neither was he inclined to give his mistress the benefit of the doubt. He ordered Three-Fingered Jack to saddle up the horses, then casually emptied the contents of his revolver, six shots, into the body of his voluptuous paramour. As she lay moaning on the floor, he sprinkled kerosene around the adobe house and then, as he departed, tossed a match into it. Incredibly, Maria Benites survived, and years later, in San Jose, where she had settled, she delighted in shucking her clothes to display the half-dozen healed bullet holes left by Murietta's bullets.

The bandit chief picked up the remnants of his horde and, skirting the coast, worked his way north. A rancher was murdered near Santa Barbara. Another ranch was raided near San Luis Obispo, with three more victims. Rumors began to circulate from one end of the state to the other that Murietta was recruiting the largest band of his career, and citizens from San Francisco to Los Angeles prepared for another siege of terror.

Governor John Bigler added a thousand-dollar reward for Murietta, dead or alive, to the other many rewards posted. The State Assembly convened at Benecia and accepted a proposal from Harry Love in southern California that he form a private company to hunt down the elusive outlaw. The solons gave him ninety days to complete the task, limited the size of the group to twenty men, and gave it the name of the California Rangers. It was at this point that the saga of Joaquin Murietta took its most bizarre twist.

The recruiting for the Rangers took place in northern California, and among the early volunteers was a young man named William Wallace Byrnes. At first, the dour Harry Love was unimpressed.

"But I am one of the few men in California who can recognize him," Byrnes said. "If you're going after Murietta, you must have someone along who can recognize him when you catch up to him."

Harry Love finally conceded that Byrnes would indeed be an asset. Thus, when the California Rangers took to the road a week later, one member of the company was the best friend Murietta ever had.

The outlaw was reported to be in San Jose when the Rangers started their campaign in June of 1853. He was staying at the ranch of Joaquin Guerra on the outskirts of the city where he murdered the proprietor of a saloon whom he thought might have recognized him. A short time later, he killed an Indian on the Guerra ranch whom he feared might betray him. The Indian was the last man known to have been murdered by the notorious outlaw.

Oddly, the chase by Harry Love's California Rangers, and

Murietta's flight, was a slow-motion affair. The Rangers arrived in Santa Clara County and leisurely set up camp the day after Murietta, with an estimated twenty men, drifted away from the Guerra ranch. Newspapers in both San Francisco and Los Angeles reported on the progress of both companies, one commenting that the bandit appeared to be "remarkably docile" on this trip. Murietta, although still traveling slowly, outdistanced the much slower moving Rangers, and by the time the bandit reached San Luis Obispo, the Rangers were still sweeping the foothills of the Santa Cruz Mountains, many miles to the north.

The California *Police Gazette* reported laconically that, while passing through San Luis Obispo, Murietta was seen conversing with an aristocratic woman of Mexican appearance. The woman was traveling by coach and, after the tryst, continued north. The bandit continued south, and the farther he traveled, the smaller dwindled his band. A posse in Santa Barbara reported it had chased the elusive outlaw to the Santa Monica Mountains outside Los Angeles before it lost him. He was next reported to have camped in the mountains southeast of San Juan Capistrano.

Meanwhile, the California Rangers were camped at San Juan Bautista, at least four hundred miles to the north. It was there that Bill Byrnes proved his value to the Rangers. He brought into camp a young, darkly beautiful woman and took her straight to Captain Harry Love.

The woman had a most interesting story for the commander of the California Rangers. Her name, she said, was Antonia La Molinera, and for a long time she had been the mistress of Joaquin Murietta. But she had become tired of the bandit, and had fled to Los Angeles with Pancho Daniels to start a new life. Murietta, she continued, had sworn to kill her, and he surely would succeed. Her only hope for happiness lay in the death of Murietta, and thus she was prepared to betray him. He was at that moment, she said, hiding in the Cantua Arroya, about two days distant to the southeast.

Bill Byrnes gravely nodded his head. La Molinera's information undoubtedly was correct. To Harry Love, her information appeared authentic, and as Bill Byrnes gallantly escorted La Molinera back to the town, Love made preparations for the showdown.

The rangers left San Juan Bautista at dawn and rode hard all day. By late the following afternoon, they were on the east side of the Coast Range, and by night, they were within sight of the narrow defile which led into Cantua Arroya. At dawn the following morning, the Rangers cautiously moved into the canyon. Around a turn, they saw the smoke of a campfire rising straight into still air from a mesa a short distance above them.

There were seven Mexicans in the camp when the Rangers galloped in. One was frying bacon over the fire. Five others were watching the cook sleepily, and the seventh was washing down the legs of his horse. The last Ranger to come up over the lip of the mesa was Bill Byrnes. He reined his mount, then suddenly pointed his finger at the Mexican by the horse. "It's Joaquin!" he cried.

The Rangers immediately opened fire. The slender man by the horse leaped onto the animal's back and, using it as a shield, raced out of the camp. One of the Rangers, William T. Henderson, went after the fleeing youth. The remainder fought point-blank with the others around the campfire and, when four of the Mexicans were killed, accepted the other two as prisoners. None of the Rangers was hurt.

Henderson caught up with his quarry some two miles farther up the canyon, bringing down first the horse and then the man. When the battle was over, the Rangers were faced with a problem. The rewards for Murietta's capture were large, but it would be a struggle to carry his body back to civilization. It was Bill Byrnes who solved the problem. "Hell, it ain't much work to pack back the head," he said, and with a hatchet and a bowie knife he severed the head of Henderson's victim and tied it to his saddle pommel. The hand of one of the victims at the campfire site, reportedly with one finger missing, also was whacked off. The rest of the bodies were left where they had fallen as, with head and hand and two prisoners, the Rangers started back. By the time they reached the first town, however, one of their prisoners was gone. Antonio Lopez, Love reported, had committed suicide by jumping into a mountain creek. The remaining prisoner, a sullen man who refused to open his mouth, made it as far as Martinez before he was taken by a mob from the Rangers' custody and strung up to a nearby tree.

The California legislature was most grateful. In addition to the reward posted by Governor Bigler and numerous other rewards posted by communities from Stockton to Los Angeles, the legislature voted an additional five-thousand-dollar bonus to the intrepid Harry Love. Henderson's share of the reward money was augmented by proceeds from a tour of the state in which the citizens, for a one-dollar fee, could see the head, the hand, and the man who killed Murietta.

Later, the head was sold at an auction for thirty-five dollars, and eventually wound up in the Barbary Coast saloon where it remained on display until it was destroyed in the disastrous earthquake and fire of 1906. No one seriously questioned its authenticity. Love was a hero, and the deeds of heroes are not questioned until they have lost their following.

The first serious doubts were raised by a San Francisco news-paperman, R. M. Daggett. Several years after the fight in Cantua Arroya, Daggett traced Byrnes to Fresno, California, and interviewed him on the anniversary of Murietta's death.

"One pickled head is as good as any other if no one knows the difference," Byrnes told Daggett. "Joaquin will have to be killed once more to entitle him to a burial."

It is a most interesting statement, inasmuch as it was Byrnes who rode into the camp of the outlaw and started the chase that led to Murietta's death . . . or someone else's death. There are some who claim that Murietta lived to be an old man back in his native state of Sonora. Among these was an aging Catholic priest in Santa Barbara who had married Antonio Murietta to his bride in Los Angeles. After reading of the death of Billy Byrnes several years later, he told a newspaperman friend that Joaquin was still alive, living in Mag-dalena, Sonora, Mexico, and that he had been given this information by Antonio.

Love died after being shot in the aftermath of a domestic squab-ble. All of the other members of his posse, except Byrnes, died violently. La Molinera disappeared, and this too is in the tale sung to a guitar.

There are some who claim that there never was a Joaquin Murietta, but this is a most difficult theory to accept. There are far too many records attesting to his existence, and newspapers of that era carried too many stories of the fearsome Mexican bandit "who plun-ders the entire state with impunity."

Whether Murietta died a young man in the foothills of the Sierra Nevada or an old man in the foothills of the Sierra Madre, his name will remain in the legends of the mysterious West for many years to come.

The outlaws wrestled one of the five-hundred-pound ingots from the freight train to the wagon. The other slab of silver was left on the train; nothing else was taken.

Tiburcio Vasquez

THERE were many gangs of bandits roaming the West after Murietta, and, with few exceptions, they were all composed of Mexicans. But where Murietta had enjoyed a certain amount of popularity, the bandits who followed encountered a growing hostility from the Mexican community.

This hostility became solid when Tiburcio Vasquez began roaming the highways and communities of California, stealing from and murdering Mexicans as readily as he did the Anglo invaders. And when Vasquez was hanged, so ended the long era of the large gangs of bandits that had started more than two hundred years earlier with the marauding El Chato.

Tiburcio Vasquez was as bloodthirsty as Joaquin Murietta, and more cunning. Little is known about his childhood. Some reports indicate that Vasquez, like Murietta, came to California from Mexico, and that he arrived in the Mother Lode country alone in his midteens. Other accounts have him being born in such diverse places as Texas, Los Angeles, Tucson, and San Bernardino. Still another reports that he was born of a Modoc Indian mother in northern California and that his father was a Mexican vaquero.

He was fifteen years old when Murietta either was killed or disappeared. He was sixteen when he attracted recognition of a sort by stealing a horse in Hornitos. He was caught some hours later, but, apparently because of his age, he was given a thrashing by his captors instead of the noose, and turned free. He promptly stole another horse, a more valuable animal this time, and rode it to Sacramento, where he sold it and dropped from sight. There was an increase in horse stealing around the Livermore Valley a few months later. At about the same time, Vasquez, never appearing to want for funds, appeared periodically in Monterey, where he spent money lavishly in the gambling casinos and the brothels.

Vasquez was a short man with a lined face. He usually wore a full mustache that curled down into a heavy beard which covered his chin. His eyes, set deep in his face, were extraordinarily narrow, and this, coupled with his heavy eyebrows, left the impression that he wore a perpetual squint. He was a loner in his youth, and a horse thief, and the chances are probably that he would have been hanged without a footnote of historical notice had he not met a Carlota Cabrera shortly after he emerged from his teens.

Carlota was the seventeen-year-old daughter of Armando Cabrera, a prominent, wealthy Mexican rancher in the Livermore Valley. It was unlikely that Carlota and Tibercio should meet. She was well educated, beautiful, and impetuous. He was semiliterate, unimaginative, and stolid. Yet they did meet, and for a brief period were in love. Carlota slipped away from her duenna on several occasions to meet with her lover, but after a while she tired of Vasquez and, with a flick of her hand, told him to move on.

Vasquez responded to his dismissal by dragging her, screaming, from her bedroom in the middle of the night. He threw her over his horse and raced away. Armando Cabrera gave chase, and caught up with the couple about dawn. The ensuing gunfight was brief. Vasquez was shot in the right arm. Armando took Vasquez's horse and gun and his beloved daughter back to Livermore. Vasquez lost considerable blood from his wound and, in his weakened condition, could barely walk when he stumbled into the camp of Juan and Miguel Garcia. The two brothers were part of a large family which lived on the receipts gained from small-time cattle rustling.

The Garcias removed the bullet from Vasquez's arm, bandaged his wound, and fed him for a few days until he had recovered his strength. Then they casually stole a horse for him to ride back to Monterey. Vasquez apparently had no trouble getting over his infatuation for Carlota, but he remained a lifelong friend of the Garcias'. A couple of months later, the two brothers followed Vasquez to Monterey, once the capital of California. During Vasquez's convalescence, he had become very interested in a project which the Garcias had proposed and described as "spectacular."

In the verdant and fertile fields of Mendocino in Sonoma County, north of San Francisco, were thousands of head of cattle. The Garcias were fascinated by the fact that this area had never been hit by a big raid. Because of this, they were convinced that it would be easier to rustle a whole herd of cattle out of Sonoma than to take a half dozen head out of the Livermore Valley. The Garcias convinced Vasquez that nine or ten men could round up a large herd and sell it for a fortune in San Francisco. Vasquez enthusiastically agreed to go along. It was not difficult for the Garcias to line up a half dozen who were not afraid of the risks of rustling. Vasquez and Miguel Garcia went to Sonoma and scouted the area. During the ensuing weeks, the rest of the rustlers arrived in Sonoma singly or in pairs.

The target of the rustlers was picked by Miguel Garcia. It was a large cattle ranch owned by a man named Jesse Houston, who had no close neighbors. The ranch was located in the most isolated section of the county. The rustlers started to work shortly after dusk. They cut out approximately a thousand head, and by dawn they had driven them several miles to the south. It is unknown how the theft was discovered so quickly, but by noon on the following day a posse had cornered the rustlers, and before dark on the following evening all of them were in the Sonoma jail awaiting trial and the cattle were back on the Houston ranch.

Vasquez and the two Garcia brothers were found guilty, and each was sentenced to five years in San Quentin Penitentiary. It was there that Vasquez met the cutthroats and desperados who were to form the nucleus of his gang. A little less than two years after he had entered San Quentin, Vasquez, accompanied by Francisco Barcenas, Garcia Rodrigues, Jose Chaves, and Alfredo Moreno, broke out of the prison. The escapees parted immediately after the breakout. Barcenas and Vasquez went to Amador County, in the heart of the Mother Lode country. Two weeks later, Vasquez was caught breaking into a grocery store in Angels Camp and returned to San Quentin. He remained there four years, three to finish his sentence for the cattle-rustling conviction and an additional year for his conviction for the attempted robbery of the grocery store. He was released in mid-1863. He went to San Francisco, where he immediately attempted to hold up a saloon. He was caught, and within a month once again was inside San Quentin. This time he remained there for seven years. When he was discharged, he drifted to Monterey. He was thirty one years old, and had spent more than thirteen years of his life in jail.

For the first few weeks after his discharge, Vasquez lived quietly in Monterey. Then Barcenas slipped into town, followed closely by Garcia Rodrigues, Miguel Garcia, and a Pedro Nuñez. A few days later, the quintet rode out of the city, and the first Vasquez gang came into existence. The first victim of the gang was a butcher employed by the New Almaden Mines near San Jose. He was stabbed to death in his home, and approximately five hundred dollars was taken. The band then followed the steps of Joaquin Murietta, drifting south to hide out in the Cantua Arroya in the mountains of the Coast Range.

It was from that point that Vasquez began to emerge from his petty-hoodlum status. Like Murietta, neither he nor his men made any attempt to keep their identities secret. They would appear suddenly at a wayside inn, rob it and all of its patrons, then ride off and disappear. A stage would be held up in northern California. The passengers would be robbed, then left face down with wrists tied to ankles. It became a Vasquez trademark. A few days later, another stage would be struck in central California, to be followed by still another Vasquez strike near Santa Barbara. Henry Sinclair Drago, in his book *Road Agents and Train Robbers,* tells of the first breakup of the Vasquez gang of outlaws.

The band held up a stage near the town of Hollister, robbing the passengers and tying them up. A short time after this, they ran across a well-dressed traveler and robbed him of more than five hundred dollars. These robberies were reported to the sheriff in Monterey, who at the time was being visited by Harry Love, the manhunter who had run Murietta down some years earlier. Love guessed correctly that Vasquez would be headed back to his hideout in the Cantua Arroya. The wily Love literally cut off the bandit gang at the pass. An ambush was set up, and in the ensuing uproar the lawmen killed Barcenas and seriously wounded Vasquez and Rodrigues. Garcia and Nuñez abandoned the two wounded men and escaped into the mountains.

Vasquez and Rodrigues managed to stay on their mounts as the posse followed the wounded men toward Santa Barbara. Three days later, an exhausted Rodrigues was found lying on his horse many miles to the south. There was no trace of Vasquez. The bandit had found a strange friend.

After leaving Rodrigues, Vasquez pushed south despite his wounds, and rode his horse to death. When the animal collapsed, Vasquez continued on foot, until he too finally was overcome by exhaustion and fell by the side of the road.

The boss teamster in southern and central California at this time was a man named Remi Nadeau. His twenty-mule freight teams with their distinctive blue wagons roamed over the southern half of the state. Nadeau built way stations where freight could be transferred and animals rested, and on more than one occasion these way stations had been robbed by bandits, including Vasquez.

Nadeau was driving his buggy from one way station to another when he came across Vasquez's dead horse. He removed the saddle and bridle from the animal and placed them in his buggy. A short time later, Nadeau drew abreast of the unconscious bandit. He manhandled the bandit into the buggy and drove to his next way station. There he gave instructions that the man be secreted and cared for until Nadeau returned. The teamster came back in a couple of weeks, gave the bandit a horse, and, according to some versions, extracted an agreement in return for his favors: Vasquez not only would not attack any Nadeau properties in the future, but he also would protect them from forays by other bandits.

An appreciative Vasquez kept his part of the agreement, with one exception. On several occasions, at a later date, his band of outlaws was seen swooping down on a Nadeau freight train, only to veer off when the distinctive blue wagons were recognized. The exception involved a raid on a Nadeau wagon carrying two five-hundred-pound ingots of silver from the notorious Panamint City to Los Angeles. The mine owners had been tipped that hijackers planned to steal the silver shipment and had cast the ingots into five-hundred-pound slabs to thwart the robbers.

The ingots were carried by buckboard from the mine to Panamint, where they were transferred to the regular Nadeau freight wagon. The buckboard was fastened to the rear of the freight wagon and towed behind for the trip to Los Angeles.

About forty miles north of Los Angeles is the Vasquez Rocks Recreation Area. These pockmarked rocks, thrust up to heights in excess of two hundred feet by temblors along the San Andreas Fault, sprawl over a large area near the southern end of the Mojave Desert. Clustered over more than one thousand acres, these rocks are as full of holes and small caves as a giant piece of wormwood. It was from this warren that Tiburcio Vasquez operated while he was in southern California.

Vasquez struck the Nadeau freight train near the rocks that bear his name. With the band was a harnessed mule, which was quickly hitched to the buckboard. The outlaws wrestled one of the five-hundred-pound ingots from the freight train to the wagon. Nothing else was taken. The buckboard and the outlaws headed for Vasquez Rocks. The freight train once again resumed its trip to Los Angeles.

The following day, a posse reached the bandits' headquarters. The buckboard was found abandoned. There was no trace of Vasquez or his outlaws. There was no doubt that Vasquez was the culprit. Mule skinners on the freight train, who were shown pictures of the bandit, identified him as the man responsible for the robbery.

After this robbery, the Vasquez band slowly drifted north. One of its members, a close associate of Tibercio Vasquez's, was a man named Manuel Moreno, whose wife was expectionally beautiful. When the bandits reached north-central California, Vasquez suggested that they break up for a short period of time and that they rendezvous in Monterey in approximately three weeks. He told

Moreno, however, to go directly to Monterey and wait for him there. Moreno and Vasquez parted, Vasquez riding to the east and Moreno riding to the west. Moreno had gone but a short distance before he decided that he would detour on his journey to Monterey and pay a visit to his wife, in Hollister. He arrived at his home shortly before dusk. Vasquez's horse was standing near the small porch. Moreno's astonishment quickly turned to anger. He burst in the front door with his gun drawn, but Vasquez apparently had seen him coming. He killed Moreno with a single shot as he came through the front door. Then, for some reason never determined, he shot Moreno's screaming wife, leaped onto his horse, and galloped out of town.

The band regrouped. By early summer in 1873, the gang was spreading terror throughout all of north-central California. It coursed erratically, robbing a stage in the morning, looting a store fifty miles away in the late afternoon. Lone travelers were systematically robbed, and sometimes murdered. Then, on August 26, came what was to be known as the Tres Piños Massacre. Tres Piños was a small town south of Hollister. Its general store was operated by a man named Arthur Snyder, and it was this store that was to be the target for the Vasquez gang.

The robbery started out in the usual routine manner of a Vasquez operation. Five bandits entered the store at intervals, and three others, including Vasquez, maintained a watch outside. Then, with pistols drawn, the bandits inside ordered the patrons and clerks, including a young boy, to lie down on the floor.

The looting of the store and the robbing of its patrons was nearly complete when a deaf sheepherder named William Redford approached the store. Vasquez ordered Redford to stop. The sheepherder, unable to hear the command, continued on. Vasquez shot him twice, killing him instantly. The sound of the gunfire brought two men running to the store. One was James Riley, a stagecoach driver. The identity of the other man is unknown, but as he ran up the stairs Vasquez hit him over the head with his gun butt, fracturing his skull. Riley turned to run, then fell dead after Vasquez shot him through the heart.

The bandit ran to his horse and pulled his rifle from its scabbard. No one knows what target Vasquez had in mind when he pulled the trigger of his rifle. The bullet tore through the wall of the Tres Pinos Hotel, more than a hundred yards distance, killing a John Davidson who was standing in the lobby. The small brother of the boy inside the store pushed his head in the back door. He was grabbed by José Chavez and brutally pistol-whipped. He died of his injuries a couple of months later.*

The massacre aroused the public's indignation. The California Assembly posted a reward of three thousand dollars for the capture of Vasquez, dead or alive, and as the pressure increased on the outlaws, they slowly moved south. Two stores in the town of Kingston were robbed. The Los Angeles-Owens Valley Stage was ambushed. A Los Angeles businessman was robbed and murdered near Tejon Pass, north of Los Angeles. The Assembly, prodded by irate newspaper editors, raised the Vasquez reward to eight thousand dollars. The size of the reward now was large enough to attract the attention of Harry Morse.

Harry Morse worked diligently at two jobs. He was Sheriff of Alameda County, near San Francisco, and he also was a professional bounty hunter. Whenever a reward for a bandit became high enough, he would leave his jurisdiction and go after his quarry, no matter where he might be hiding. On some occasions he was given expense money by the state for his hunts, and because of his political connections, Morse was not challenged by Alameda County officials for his long and frequent absences. He captured the notorious Manuel Flores in a remote mountain cabin near Fresno. A short time later, he trailed and captured the psychotic killer-bandit Juan Soto after he had slaughtered Newell Tice and his family near San Luis Obispo.

Now Vasquez became his quarry. Using his political connections, Morse obtained a commitment from the State Assembly to finance his expedition. He put together a small posse of tough gunmen and followed the Vasquez trail to the south. Two members of the Morse band were Mexicans. They had little difficulty in picking up information, because Vasquez had no friends in the Mexican community.

---

*Anyone searching for traces of this shootout will be unable to find them in present-day Tres Piños. The massacre occurred in what is now known as Paicines, some five miles south of the current Tres Piños. The Southern Pacific Railroad planned to use Tres Piños as a terminal point, and a post office was established there. Because of engineering difficulties, however, the railroad terminal was moved to a point five miles from the community. The post office was moved to the railroad depot about three years after the massacre, and it kept the name Tres Piños. A small community built up there, and to avoid confusion, the residents of the original Tres Piños changed the name of their town to Paicines.

Vasquez's existence was humiliating to the Mexicans, and most wanted him quickly caught and hanged.

A couple of months after the Tres Pinos Massacre, Vasquez and two members of his gang appeared at the ranch of Alessandro Repetto, nine miles from Los Angeles in what is now Hollywood. Repetto, whose reputation was somewhat questionable, was not happy to see the notorious outlaw. On their last visit they had remained for a week before departing with one of his best horses. This time Vasquez wanted more than a horse. "Give me eight hundred dollars," he demanded.

"I don't have it," Repetto protested.

"Then write a check."

Repetto did as he was told. A boy who worked on the ranch was sent into Los Angeles to cash it. Some time after the youth had left the bank, the banker became suspicious of the transaction and notified Los Angeles Sheriff William Rowland. The sheriff did not think the matter an urgent one, and so a couple of days passed before a deputy stopped by the Repetto ranch to check on the transaction.

Vasquez and his companions had left, and Repetto fearfully identified his extortionist as the notorious bandit. It was the first word Rowland had received that Vasquez was operating that close to Los Angeles.

Meanwhile, Morse and his posse had reached Vasquez Rocks, which, according to informants, was the southern headquarters for the gang. For about a week, the posse remained out of sight near the rocks, looking for some sign of the bandit. When none was forthcoming, Morse sent the two Mexican members of the posse on into Los Angeles to search for information. These two lawmen posed as desperados, and finally, in a barrio cantina, they picked up a tip that the Vasquez gang was scattering and that Vasquez and Chavez were hiding at a ranch in the Cahuenga Hills owned by a George Allen.

According to Drago, when this information was passed on to Morse, he rode into Los Angeles to pay a courtesy call on Los Angeles Sheriff Rowland. It was Morse's intention to allow Rowland to participate in the capture. Rowland wanted no part of Morse, but he did want the reward money. He told Morse that he had had the Allen ranch under surveillance and that if Morse knew what was good for him, he would get himself and his men out of Los Angeles County immediately.

Although Morse was funded by the state, he did not want to have a confrontation with Rowland. The Alameda sheriff gathered up his men and rode north. Rowland immediately formed a posse. One of its members was George Beers, the Los Angeles correspondent for the San Francisco *Chronicle*.

It was shortly after noon when the Rowland posse arrived in the vicinity of the Allen ranch. For a while the men remained out of sight as they debated various plans for storming the house. While they were so engaged, a man working on the ranch came along in a mule-drawn buckboard. He confirmed that Vasquez was in the house. Chavez had left two days earlier, saying that he was going to Mexico.

In the back of the buckboard was a large canvas. Beers and a deputy sheriff, Johnny Johnson, crawled under the canvas and told the driver to go straight to the front entrance of the adobe ranch house. The driver did as he was told.

A few moments later, Beers and Johnson leaped out of the buckboard and charged into the house. Johnson was immediately tackled by Allen's mistress, and his rifle went off as he fell to the floor. Beers jumped over the wrestling couple and ran to the rear of the house. Vasquez was halfway through a window when Beers saw him. The reporter fired his shotgun, and Vasquez was brought down, his legs riddled with buckshot.

It was nearly the end for Vasquez. He was taken to Los Angeles jail, where he was held on two murder warrants in connection with the slaying of Redford and Davidson in Tres Pinos. Vasquez had sufficient funds to hire a competent attorney, who successfully won a change of venue for the trial from San Benito County to San Jose, in Santa Clara County. The trial there lasted four days. On January 9, 1875, Vasquez was found guilty of the murders and sentenced to be hanged.

Shortly before the hanging took place, Vasquez had a visitor, Remi Nadeau. "I thought we had an arrangement," Nadeau said.

Vasquez spread out his palms. "There was a problem," he said. "I have a cousin who is a card dealer in Panamint. It was he who told me of the bullion shipment, and I had an obligation to him. But I am also your friend, Remito. I owe to you my life. That is why I took only one of the ingots. I put it in a hole in the rocks. Do you understand?"

Nadeau was not sure that he did.

Sheriff Rowland of Los Angeles collected the eight-thousand-dollar reward. George Beers had a sensational story in the San Francisco *Chronicle*.

On March 19, 1875, Vasquez was hanged in San Jose, his death bringing to an end the gangs of Mexican bandits that had plagued California for a quarter of a century.

This was the last that was ever heard from Black Bart.
Never again did he jump in front of a stage wearing
his ghostly garb, but his apprehension became
an obsession with Hume.

Black Bart, The PO-8

I've labored long and hard for bread
For honor and for riches
But on my corns too long you've tread
You fine haired sons of bitches.
                    BLACK BART, PO-8

It was on a pleasant early summer day in 1875 when Black Bart, the

49

the PO-8, made his first spectacular appearance in the first of a long series of stage holdups. Before he disappeared, more than a decade later, he had become a legend in California, a sort of Robin Hood to all who hated the powerful Wells Fargo Company and a symbol of anarchy to the establishment of the times.

The first robbery occurred on Funck Hill near the foothill town of Milton in Calaveras County in northern California. Driver of the Sonora-Milton stage on that day was John "Cappy" Shine. He had been on that run for a little more than three years, and he was well used to driving the swaying stage over the switchbacks on the steep grade. About midway down the hill, the lead horse shied as it entered a turn. Cappy Shine abruptly braked the vehicle and reined the animals to a halt. As the dust settled, a strange apparition slowly moved out from behind a huge boulder.

It wore an ankle-length linen duster that was soiled and crumpled. Over its head was a clean white flour sack in which two holes had been cut, through which Cappy Shine could see two brilliant blue eyes staring up at him. Two gloved hands held a double-barreled shotgun, the muzzles pointed directly at Cappy Shine's chest. "Keep your eyes on them, boys, and be ready with both barrels," the apparition said in a deep, resonant voice.

A female passenger inside the stage began to scream. Cappy Shine looked past the bandit. Several gun barrels pointed at the stage from behind other boulders scattered up the side of the hill.

"Throw down the money box," the bandit said calmly. Then, turning his head toward the passenger compartment of the stage, he called out, "Dear lady. You can stop screaming, for absolutely no harm will befall you, nor will you suffer any loss of your possessions."

It is not known how the woman heard the bandit over her wails, but the screaming stopped. Cappy Shine lifted the wooden Wells Fargo money box from the top of the stage and tossed it over the side. The bandit motioned with his gun for Cappy Shine to move on. As the stage neared the next switchback on the trail, Cappy Shine looked back over his shoulder. The bandit, still wearing his ghostly costume and still protected by his hidden companions, was hacking the money box to splinters with a small axe.

As soon as Cappy Shine reached the bottom of the steep grade, he lathered the horses to the next stage depot, in Reynolds Ferry. From there, a man was dispatched back to Copperopolis to notify the sheriff, who wired news of the holdup to Wells Fargo headquarters, in San Francisco. A relief driver replaced Cappy Shine on the stage. Cappy waited for the sheriff in Reynolds Ferry, who arrived in the early afternoon.

The sheriff was puzzled. He had heard nothing about a band of outlaws operating in the area. From Cappy Shine's description of the size of the gang, it would require a very large posse indeed to pursue it. Additionally, many hours had passed since the holdup, making a chase virtually hopeless. The sheriff, a deputy, and Cappy Shine went to the scene of the crime on Funck Hill.

The shattered money box lay in the middle of the stage trail, its contents gone. Oddly, one of the rifle barrels Cappy Shine had seen earlier still projected over the boulder, although now it no longer appeared menacing. Cappy Shine climbed up the side of the hill to it, then swore loudly. The "rifle barrel" was a stick. A quick search discovered similar sticks. The size of the gang dwindled to one man.

Cappy Shine returned to the dummy rifle that had been left in place, and this time he noticed a piece of ruled paper pinned between the wood and the small crevice in which it was lodged. He picked it up. Penned in a slightly shaky Spencerian script was the following doggerel:

> *I've labored long and hard for bread*
> *For honor and for riches*
> *But on my corns too long you've tread*
> *You fine haired sons of bitches.*
> BLACK BART, PO-8

Laughing, Cappy Shine slid back down the hill and gave the verse to the sheriff. "There was no gang," he said after the sheriff read the doggerel. "Just a crazy poet."

"One man and on foot," the sheriff replied. "Your crazy poet didn't even have a horse. There's not a sign of one around except for those on the stage trail. You sure he had a gun?"

At this time, the Wells Fargo Bank maintained a rather large private police force. Although it was paid by a private company, in many instances it was more powerful than the public law-enforcement agencies. Its agents arrested suspects without warrants, and often transported prisoners hundreds of miles for trial within the legal jurisdiction of the alleged crimes. The worst offense that could be committed against Wells Fargo was a stage holdup in which a Wells

Fargo money box was taken. No matter how small the loot, no expense was cut in tracking down the culprit.

The take from Black Bart's robbery on Funck Hill was small, less than two hundred dollars. Nevertheless, when the report of the holdup reached the of fice of J. B. Hume, the Wells Fargo Superintendent of Investigations in San Francisco, he immediately sent a detective to the scene. Hume had formerly been a detective with the New York Police Department, and had been with Wells Fargo for about ten years when Black Bart made his debut. He dressed impeccably. He was tall and wiry. His mustache curled over thin lips that never smiled, and there were some who swore that his jet-black eyes penetrated deeply enough to read a suspect's mind. Hume saw nothing humorous in the verse left behind by the bandit, and he was skeptical about Cappy Shine's role in the incident.

This suspicion was not allayed when the detective reported back to him that Cappy Shine thought the poem was very funny, that the idea of being held up by a crazy poet was equally hilarious, and that the only description he could give of the bandit was that he had a deep voice, that his movements might be those of a middle-aged man, and that he spoke like an educated man. Shine was brought to San Francisco and interrogated by Hume, but the superintendent could not shake the driver's humorous attitude toward the holdup or his logical explanation that the reason he could not describe the bandit was because he had been all covered up.

Cappy Shine was crossed from Hume's suspect list a few weeks later when a southbound stage running from San Juan to Marysville was held up at a point more than one hundred fifty miles from Funck Hill. The bandit fit precisely the description of Black Bart. He wore a soiled, ankle-length linen duster, and a flour sack over his head with holes cut out for his sight. His eyes were a piercing blue, and his voice articulate and resonant. This time, however, he did not pretend to be commanding a gang. He leaped out from behind a boulder, pointed a shotgun toward the driver, and shouted for the stage to halt. When his instructions were followed, he took partial shelter behind the lead horse and ordered that the Wells Fargo money box be thrown down. Again, when the stage was told to proceed, the driver looked over his shoulder and saw the bandit smashing the money box to bits with a hatchet. When the deputies arrived on the scene a few hours later, they found a note. "Driver, give my respects to our friend, the other driver; but I really had a notion to hang my hat on his weather eye. Respectfully, B.B."

This time, Hume sent his top investigator, Harry Morse, to the scene. Morse had left his job as Alameda County Sheriff shortly after the capture of Tiburcio Vasquez. The Spencerian handwriting on the note left behind appeared similar to that of the doggerel at Funck Hill. There was no sign of a horse used by the bandit. There were several scattered ranches in the vicinity of the holdup, but no one working on them could recall any stranger worthy of note. Morse did locate a farmer who had passed the holdup site in a buckboard about fifteen minutes earlier, but this man had neither seen nor heard anything unusual. Morse returned to San Fancisco.

The loot in the second robbery was a little higher than in the first; about five hundred dollars in gold coin and a little less in postal certificates. Hume had Wells Fargo post a reward of three hundred dollars for information leading to the arrest and conviction of the bandit known as Black Bart. He also got California Governor William Irwin to match the reward. The U.S. Post Office Department added another two hundred dollars.

Five months passed before Black Bart struck again. This time he hit the southbound express from Roseburg, Oregon, in a mountainous area more than five hundred miles north of San Francisco. His *modus operandi* was identical to that of his other operations. His garb was the same, the linen duster and the flour sack. This time, in addition to the money box, he took the mail sack, which he ripped open in a T slash with a sharp knife. The doggerel he left behind in the ruins of the splintered money box was different.

> *I've travelled many a mile*
> *To meet with you today*
> *And I leave you with a smile*
> *As I take your money away.*
> BLACK BART, PO-8

Again Hume sent Harry Morse to investigate, and again the story was the same. This time the loot, however, was more than one thousand dollars; it was the first time this amount of gold had ever been carried on that stage.

Morse roamed the countryside looking for possible witnesses, and about a week after his arrival he came up with the first possible lead to Black Bart. About twenty miles from the scene of the holdup, the detective came across a sheepherder who had indeed seen an odd stranger about dusk on the day of the robbery. The sheepherder was preparing his evening meal when the stranger arrived and asked for a cup of coffee. He was invited to share the sheepherder's meal, but declined. He did, however, consume an entire pot of coffee while his host ate. The sheepherder described the stranger to the detective as being a little under six feet, with no excess weight. He wore a full white mustache and long, full sideburns.

"What was there about him that struck you as odd?" Morse asked.

"It was the manner in which he dressed. Here we are miles from the nearest building of any sort, yet the stranger was dressed as if he were in the center of a city," the shepherd replied. "He wore a derby hat, a double-breasted coat, and he carried a large and apparently heavy valise." The only part of the stranger's wardrobe that agreed with the environment was the pair of comfortable boots. The stranger had volunteered no information about himself, and the shepherd had asked for none. The conversation had been limited to problems encountered in raising sheep. After resting about an hour, the stranger had picked up his valise and strode off to the south.

Morse made extensive notes on the sheepherder's story, but within the next week was unable to find anyone else who had encountered the traveler in the strange garb. He also heard tales from other residents in the area that the shepherd was "a bit balmy." The detective returned to San Francisco.

A little more than six months passed before Black Bart surfaced again, this time near Fort Ross, a fishing village founded by the Russians approximately one hundred miles north of San Francisco. As the stage rounded a bend in the trail a few miles east of the village, a "scarecrow" dressed in a linen duster and white leggings, with a flour sack pulled over his head, stepped out from behind a boulder and leveled a shotgun at the driver's head. Again the highwayman asked for the mail sack in addition to the Wells Fargo Express box. The driver noticed some other "guns" pointed in his direction from behind rocks farther up the hill, and quickly obeyed the bandit's orders.

A woman passenger in the stagecoach threw out her purse. The bandit turned his attention away from the driver, walked over to the purse, and picked it up. "My dear woman," he said as he tossed the purse back into the stage. "With me, your valuables are as safe as your virtue. I take only from Wells Fargo and the Government." He then motioned for the stage to move on, and as the driver looked back, he saw the oddly dressed bandit hacking away at the money box with a hatchet.

The sheriff who arrived on the scene a couple of hours later found the "guns" to be sticks. The mail bag had been slit apart. Written on the back of an envelope and tucked under the splintered money box was the following:

> *It is when a man is in his prime*
> *And finds himself a clerk*
> *That to profit he must turn to crime*
> *And make it his life's work.*
>
> BLACK BART PO-8

So it went. The file on Black Bart thickened in the San Francisco offices of Wells Fargo. The bandit appeared every five or six months, made his haul, then vanished. Black Bart did not always leave a poem behind, but he usually left some sort of note in order that no imposter might don his flour sack and duster. The loot varied from as low as a hundred fifty dollars to slightly more than five thousand dollars. Black Bart was becoming a legend. Songs were being sung in the saloons about his exploits. Road shows put on skits extolling the bandit who robbed only Wells Fargo and had never hurt a soul. Newspapers questioned the competency of the highly publicized Wells Fargo police. Hume was stymied. The closest thing he had in his files as a clue to Black Bart was the sheepherder's description. And that, in all probability, was a description of some innocent traveler.

Black Bart roamed all over northern California. For the first four years, he spaced his robberies carefully as to both time and place. Then he changed his *modus operandi,* striking rapidly at three stages in as many days in the vicinity of Oroville. Hume rushed Morse and two other detectives into the area, and this time Morse found a couple of witnesses who looked good. Near the Eel River, not far distant from Oroville, Morse came across a small, isolated ranch operated by a widow named Mrs. Jack McCready and her unusually observant sixteen-year-old daughter, Maxine. They told Morse the following story:

A couple of days before the first in the series of three robberies, a gentleman tourist had arrived at the farm, seeking directions to Oroville. Visitors were rare in that area, and when Mrs. McCready asked him to remain for a noonday lunch, the stranger accepted graciously. He did not volunteer his name. He spoke courteously in a deep voice. Maxine reported that his coat sleeve bore a tear which had been mended with white thread. One of his shoes had been split with a knife under the ball of the foot. His watch chain had broken and been repaired with a leather thong. His hair was brown turning gray, thinning above the forehead with slight balding at the temples. His eyes were deep-set, a piercing blue, under tufted eyebrows. His hands were slender and genteel. He did not smoke or drink liquor, but consumed several cups of coffee, before, during, and after his meal. He spoke well and fluently, and carried on an intellectual conversation. He also had a keen sense of humor, and had the two women laughing during most of his visit. He told them nothing about himself.

"Did he have a hat?" Morse asked.

"A derby."

"Sideburns and a mustache?"

Maxine nodded. "The sideburns were thick and white," she replied. "The mustache was cut in the imperial style."

Morse had one more question. "Did he carry a valise?"

The stranger had carried two, one large and with a hand grip, the other smaller and slung over his shoulder by a strap. Morse felt a wild surge of elation. The description corresponded to that offered by the sheepherder far to the north. At long last, after all these years, he finally had a rough description of Black Bart. Morse returned to Oroville. The sheriff had a new poem for him, left behind from a new holdup in the area to the east of the community on the Quincy stage route.

> *Here I lay me down to sleep*
> *To wait the coming morrow*
> *Perhaps success, perhaps defeat*
> *And everlasting sorrow*
> *Let come what will, I'll try it on*
> *My condition can't be worse*
> *And if there's money in that box*
> *'Tis munney in my purse.*

This holdup was less than three hours old, and, so far as Morse knew, never had a Wells Fargo detective been so close to the elusive bandit. Morse rode with the posse out to the holdup scene, but Black Bart had left no trail. The detective spent ten days searching the area for possible witnesses, but there were none. This robbery was one of the most profitable: about five thousand dollars, including a two-thousand-dollar diamond ring.

The ubiquitous Black Bart fell back into his old pattern of one holdup at a time, usually spaced about five months apart and at widely scattered locations, ranging as far north as the Oregon border. In every instance during the ensuing four years, Morse visited the scene of the robbery, searching for witnesses or clues. There were none. No one, other than the McCreadys and the sheepherder, could be found who had seen him. The reward money for Black Bart's apprehension had now swelled to ten thousand dollars, but all Hume could tell his frustrated superiors was "We have a good idea of what he looks like, and we'll catch him eventually."

November is usually chilly in the foothills of northern California. Milton, in Calaveras County, was a foothill town, near Funck Hill, where Black Bart had made his debut. In the eight years since then, Milton had grown slightly. Now two stage lines crossed at Milton, and the stage depot there was a collecting point for passengers traveling to and from San Francisco via Stockton.

The morning of November 3, 1883, was clear and cold. Frost covered the thick scrub oak and mistletoe in many areas of the county, and the ponds and lakes were covered with thin ice. Reason E. McConnell was a driver for the Nevada Stage Company. On this day, he started his trip in Sonora at four A.M. in order to make the necessary connections with the other stages at Milton. At six thirty A.M. he arrived in Reynolds Ferry, where he discharged two passengers and was supposed to pick up three more. None of the three passengers was present in the stage depot, so McConnell walked over to the town's only hotel to see if they were awaiting him there. No one there knew of them. McConnell decided he could wait for a while, as he had no other passengers on this day. His cash box, which had been bolted to the stagecoach frame through the floor, contained more than five thousand dollars' worth of gold dust being shipped from the Patterson Mine to Wells Fargo in San Francisco, about five hundred dollars' worth of gold coins, and an undetermined amount of amalgam. McConnell had no idea of the contents of his cash box, however, and, with no passengers, he felt no urgency in making his connection in Milton.

He ordered a cup of coffee and struck up a conversation with Jimmy Rolleri, the nineteen-year-old son of the hotel owner. About a half-hour later, when McConnell stood up to go, Jimmy asked if he could ride on the stage as far as Copperopolis.

"Sure, but how do you plan on getting back?"

"I won't go all the way," Jimmy said. "I'll probably get off the other side of Funck Hill and do some hunting on my way back."

When the stage departed Reynolds Ferry, man and boy were riding on top of it. Jimmy carried an old Henry single-shot rifle with him. McConnell was unarmed. For about an hour, the steel-rimmed wheels of the stage crunched brittlely over the frozen ground on the trail, before it came to the first of the switchbacks that wound the trail over Funck Hill. The grade was sufficiently steep to force the horses to a slow walk. Jimmy, carrying his rifle, jumped off. "I'm going to do some hunting," he said, "and I'll meet you on the other side." He scampered off into the thick scrub oak and disappeared.

The heavy stage creaked its way slowly up the steep hill. About halfway to the top, as the lead horse turned in to another switchback, the familiar apparition, enshrouded in flour sack and linen duster, leaped from behind a large boulder. Gloved hands held a shotgun pointed at McConnell's head.

McConnell wrestled with the reins and swore at the nervous horses. Like every other stage driver in northern California, he knew of Black Bart. His first thought was of the possible adverse reaction from the bandit when he was told there was no Wells Fargo box to throw down, that it had been bolted to the floor of the stage as a security measure.

Instead of immediately demanding the box, however, the legendary bandit asked, "Who jumped off the stage down below?"

McConnell, still quieting the horses, did not reply, and Black Bart did not press him. The bandit waited patiently until the animals were quiet, then ordered McConnell to throw down the money box.

McConnell explained why he could not, and when he finished, he suddenly had the impression that Black Bart was uncertain of his next move. For a long moment, the two men stared at each other. Then Black Bart sighed. "Get down," he said.

"I can't," McConnell replied. "The hand brake is broken and the stage will roll back." He pointed to his foot, clamped firmly on the foot brake.

"Get down and put a rock behind the wheel."

The fear began to leave the stage driver. "You put the rock behind the wheel," he replied.

Black Bart shrugged slightly. Then, holding his shotgun loosely in the crook of his arm, he walked to the rear of the coach. Presently he found a large rock at the side of the trail, which he wedged with his foot against the wheel. His movements were becoming more nervous. McConnell thought he knew why. Previously, Black Bart had had the strongbox in his possession and the stage under way in less than five minutes. Today, almost that amount of time had passed and the box still was secure inside the stage. Also, the bandit knew that there was an armed man somewhere in the vicinity—another situation that he had never faced before.

"Now get down," Black Bart ordered.

McConnell complied and stood beside his horses.

"Unhitch 'em and drive them over the hill."

Jimmy Rolleri greeted McConnell with wide-open eyes when he drove his team of stageless horses over the crest of Funck Hill a short time later. McConnell explained the situation in two words. "Black Bart," he said. It took less than a moment for the man and the boy to reach a decision on their course of action. With the help of Jimmy's ancient rifle, they would capture the notorious Black Bart.

Stealthily, the two worked their way down the hill through the thick scrub oak. They soon heard the sound of pounding, and then, when they drew in sight of the stagecoach, they could see the outline of the cavalier bandit inside the vehicle, splintering the strongbox with his small axe. The pair paused. More than a half-hour had passed since Black Bart had appeared. The box, McConnell thought, must have been reinforced by metal to withstand such a pounding for so long. Jimmy raised his rifle, but McConnell depressed the barrel with his hand. "Let's get closer," he whispered.

Silently, man and boy worked their way down the hill. When they were within fifty yards of the coach, they paused again. At that moment, the bandit backed out of the stage, the sacks of gold clutched to his chest. As Black Bart straightened and picked up his shotgun, Jimmy fired. The bullet struck the stage, missing the bandit by several feet, but the sound of the shot had an electrifying effect on Black

Bart. Without a glance to see from where the shot came, Black Bart raced down the trail with the speed of a startled hare, his linen duster streaming in the air behind him. Then, as Jimmy was reloading his ancient weapon, Black Bart suddenly bounded off into the woods and disappeared. Jimmy fired two more rounds in the general direction of the fugitive crashing through the woods, but neither he nor McConnell made any attempt to follow. They could be ambushed much too easily in the thick scrub. They remained hidden in the woods above the stage for a long time, until they were convinced that Black Bart was not coming back. Then they went back up the hill, retrieved the horses, harnessed them to the stage, and drove on into Copperopolis, where they reported the robbery to Sheriff Benjamin Thorne.

In the early afternoon, Thorne arrived at the scene of the holdup with a small posse. Near the point where Black Bart had turned in to the woods, he found a flour sack with two eyeholes cut into it. A few feet farther down the hill, he picked up a brown derby hat. Behind the large boulder where Black Bart had lain in wait Thorne found a mass of evidence. There the bandit had abandoned a leather case for field glasses, a belt, a magnifying glass, a razor, a handkerchief formed into a pouch which contained buckshot, two flour sacks and two paper bags containing food staples. Printing on the bags and a sales slip inside one of them indicated that the groceries had been purchased the preceding day from a store in Angels Camp, about twelve miles distant. The posse scoured the area for most of the afternoon, but Black Bart once again had vanished.

Harry Morse, the Wells Fargo detective, arrived in Copperopolis the following day and went over the evidence with the sheriff. It was Morse who noticed the laundry mark in the corner of the handkerchief made into a pouch. Clearly legible, it read "F.X.O.7." The sheriff voiced no objections to Morse's taking the handkerchief. The detective on the next day went to Angels Camp. There he talked to the proprietor of the grocery store, who recalled selling the groceries to a stranger. His description of the buyer matched that given by the McCreadys and the sheepherder.

"I can tell you something more," the proprietor added. "I saw the same man again here in Angels Camp yesterday morning. He was getting on the Stockton stage."

The detective telegraphed police in Stockton and San Francisco the information the store owner had given him, then returned to the holdup area for his customary search for possible witnesses. He found one. About three miles from the bottom of Funck Hill, there lived in a small cabin a recluse named Henry Martin. He reported that he had heard gunfire in the distance, and about three quarters of an hour later a man had passed his cabin, walking rapidly. Martin had hailed him. The man had waved back and asked if he was headed in the right direction for Angels Camp. Martin had assured him that he was, and the stranger had strode on. The description matched the others.

"How was he dressed?" Morse asked.

"In city clothes. He wore no hat, and he carried a large valise."

About six miles from Angels Camp, Harry Morse found still another witness. A "Doc" Sylvester had been returning to his home in Nassau Valley when he had been hailed by a hatless but otherwise "well-dressed" man and asked for directions to Angels Camp. Again the description matched. But no one in Angels Camp, other than the grocer, remembered the man. The stage arrived in Stockton before police received Morse's telegram, and there was no sign of the elusive Black Bart on board any of the river steamers arriving in San Francisco from Stockton.

There were approximately one hundred laundries in San Francisco, and probably three times that number scattered throughout the state, and, Hume decided, every one of them would be checked, if necessary, to find out who matched up with the laundry mark on the handkerchief left behind by Black Bart. Aside from the few descriptions, the handkerchief was the first solid lead that Wells Fargo had found after more than eight years of being victimized. He assigned almost every detective on the payroll to cover the laundries in San Francisco. On the second day of the search, a detective named Thacker discovered the laundry mark "F.X.O.7" in the records of a small company operated by A. B. Ware at 316 Bush Street.

Thacker reported the discovery personally to Hume. "It is registered to a C. E. Bolton who lives in Room Forty at the Webb House at Thirty-seven Second Street."

Less than an hour later, Hume, Morse, and Thacker arrived at the Webb House. The proprietor was cooperative, and the legal formalities of today were not so strictly observed more than a century ago. "Mr. Bolton has been with us for more than eight years," the proprietor said as he led the detectives to Bolton's room. "He is one of our best tenants. I believe he once was a schoolteacher back in the Midwest, but now he is a mining capitalist." The proprietor went on to say that Bolton frequently was gone for several days while he checked on his mining interests in the Mother Lode country. In fact, he had just returned from such a trip.

Bolton was not in his room, but the proprietor let the three men into it. There were three large empty suitcases in the room. The closet contained half a dozen fashionable suits and three derby hats. Socks, underwear, and shirts were laid out neatly in a bureau. Toilet articles were lined up on top of a small washstand. There was, however, something peculiar about the room. It gave the appearance of having just been occupied. For a man who had lived there for eight years, there was only one item of a personal nature, a Bible with the following inscription on its flyleaf: "This precious Bible is presented to Charles E. Boles, First Sergeant, Company B. 116th Illinois Volunteer Infantry, by his wife as a New Year's gift. Decatur, Illinois, 1865."

Hume turned to the proprietor. "How often is he gone for several days?" he asked.

"He's very active. Sometimes he is gone only three or four days a week. Other times he doesn't come back here for two or three weeks."

Hume checked the laundry mark on shirts and underwear. It was the same, "F.X.O.7." "This probably is just a front address," he said to Morse and Thacker. "You stay here for a while. I'm going to the laundry to see if they might have another address."

The Ware Laundry was a small operation. The front of the shop consisted only of a small entrance, a counter, and shelves on which the laundry bundles were stacked. There was a customer in the shop when Hume arrived, and the detective, after no more than a passing glance at the man's back, waited courteously until he had departed before approaching Ware. "I know Mr. Bolton has his laundry done here," he said, "and I wonder if you could tell me if he has been in recently."

Ware, a small mouse of a man, chuckled softly. "Yes, he has," he replied presently. "In fact, that was Mr. Bolton who just left."

Hume reacted swiftly. "Would you be so kind as to ask him to return. I have a mining deal in which he will be interested."

Ware ran out of the door. Hume followed him. Bolton was less than a half block away, strolling casually. At Ware's hail, he paused, turned, and slowly walked back. Hume studied the man as he approached. Long thick white sideburns curled from beneath a brown derby hat. Eyebrows were tufted and white over piercing blue eyes. His mustache was white and cut in the waterfall style. He was well dressed and carried a small cane. A stickpin with a large diamond held his tie, and on his little finger he wore a ring with an equally large diamond. A heavy gold watch chain arched across his waist. His shoulders were broad, and he carried himself erectly.

Hume held out his hand. "My name is Hamilton," he said. "I have a mining-business matter I'd like to discuss with you."

Bolton was friendly. "I'm always interested in a matter of business."

The conversation was overheard by Ware, who related it to reporters later, but what went on between Hume and Bolton during the next thirty minutes is unknown. It is known, however, that in some manner Hume enticed Bolton into an interrogation room in the Wells Fargo headquarters. Approximately six hours later, San Francisco police were summoned and Bolton was arrested on suspicion of stage robbery and taken to the city jail.

"What is your name?" the desk sergeant asked.

"T. Z. Spaulding," Bolton replied, and that was the name under which he was booked.

In less than an hour, word leaked to the press that the legendary Black Bart had been captured, and the jail swarmed with reporters. Bolton was delighted to talk with them. "If, after eight years of searching, I am the closest thing to a suspect that Wells Fargo can come up with, then the Wells Fargo police force is indeed a most inefficient and corrupt organization. Someone allegedly found a handkerchief with my laundry mark upon it at the scene of the crime. If this is true, then it is a handkerchief that was picked up after it either was discarded or lost. I am a capitalist and mining man, and my reputation, gentlemen, is impeccable. I plan to consult with an attorney tomorrow with the intent of seeking legal redress against Wells Fargo."

Hume, however, had no intention of allowing his case to become entangled by legalistics. At five the following morning, Hume and Morse took Bolton from the jail to the Embarcadero, and before the sun rose the trio was en route to Stockton. On arrival, Bolton was lodged in the city jail under the name of B. Black. He was kept in an isolated cell. Two days later, Sheriff Benjamin Thorne arrived with the hermit, Henry Martin. Bolton was pointed out in his cell to the recluse, who promptly identified him as the man who had asked for directions to Angels Camp shortly after McConnell was held up.

Bolton was next taken to Milton, where he was displayed before McConnell. The stage driver pointed out the difficulty in recognizing Bolton because the bandit had worn a flour sack over his head.

"How about his voice?" Hume asked.

McConnell accepted the hint. "It's the same voice," he agreed.

"Doc" Sylvester was the next witness to confront Bolton. When Sylvester first entered the sheriff's office where Bolton was being held, Bolton was sitting with Harry Morse. "That's him," Sylvester said, pointing to Morse. When the error was pointed out to him, he properly identified Bolton.

Apparently, no further identification was thought necessary. The grocer in Angels Camp, the McCreadys, and the sheepherder were forgotten. Bolton was taken to the county jail in San Andreas, where Hume and Morse began interrogating him again at seven P.M. At two A.M. the following morning, Bolton suddenly sighed and stood up. "I'm sleepy," he said. "If I confess, will you let me get some sleep?"

"Of course," said Hume. "Providing you return whatever loot you have not spent."

"There's not much. Although I lived modestly, Wells Fargo was my only source of income," Bolton said sadly. "All that is left are the proceeds from our last transaction."

Hume paused and rubbed his eyes. "Who are you?" he asked presently. "What is your real name? Where do you really live?"

"I am Black Bart, PO-8, and at the moment I am living in the San Andreas jail."

Hume asked the question again, but the cavalier bandit would say no more.

The following afternoon, Bolton led the two detectives to a hiding spot in a hollow log about a mile off the stage trail where he had dodged the unsure aim of Jimmy Rolleri's rifle. All but two hundred dollars' worth of the booty was recovered. That evening, he was back in jail in San Andreas.

The trial, held the following morning, was brief even by Western standards. At nine A.M., Bolton stood before Judge William Hooker and pleaded guilty to one count of armed robbery. Judge Hooker accepted the plea and sentenced Bolton to six years in San Quentin

Penitentiary. At nine thirty A.M., Bolton was en route to the state prison.

The San Francisco *Examiner* accused Hume of making a deal with Bolton, but Hume denied it, and Bolton would neither confirm nor deny it.

Black Bart served a little more than five years of his sentence. He was released on January 21, 1888, and disappeared. On July 27, the stage from Beilger to Redding was held up by a man with a flour sack over his head who escaped with more than $1,000. On November 8, a similar holdup of a stage between Downieville and Nevada City netted the bandit $2,200 worth of gold. On December 1, a man with a flour-sack mask took $700 from a Wells Fargo stage traveling between Ukiah and Eureka.

BLACK BART STRIKES AGAIN, bannered the *Territorial Enterprise,* and the exploits of the bandit were recalled by newspapers as far east as Chicago. A furious Hume was in Downieville when, a week later, Black Bart hit another stage, near Benecia. This time the loot was less than a hundred dollars, but Black Bart had taken up his pen again. The posse that arrived on the scene a few hours after the holdup found the following doggerel:

> *So here I've stood while wind and rain*
> *Have set the trees a-sobbing*
> *And risked my life for this damn stage*
> *That wasn't worth the robbing.*
> BLACK BART, PO-8

This was the last that was ever heard from Black Bart. Never again did he jump in front of a stage wearing his ghostly garb, but his apprehension became an obsession with Hume. Thousands of dollars of Wells Fargo funds were spent tracking down leads to the bandit, including one trip to Mexico City, but all were to no avail. Hume went to Decatur, Illinois, where he learned that Charles E. Boles, whose name was inscribed on the flyleaf of the Bible, had been killed in a farming accident about three years before Black Bart made his first appearance on Funck Hill. The only record Hume ever could find of the name C. E. Bolton was in the register at Webb House and the Ware Laundry. Hume even spent weeks hunting for a T. Z. Spaulding. He found nothing. This time Black Bart with all of his aliases had vanished forever.

Several years after Black Bart's last robbery, the San Francisco *Examiner* printed a story that he was living quietly in Montana, a reformed man, repentant of his sins. A few days later, the same newspaper published the following reply from Ambrose Bierce:

> *What's that? You ne'er again will rob a stage?*
> *What? Did you so? Faith, I didn't know it.*
> *Was this what threw poor Themis in a rage?*
> *I thought you were convicted as a poet.*

The vigilantes disarmed the three men and marched
them to the gallows that Plummer had built as
a warning to outlaws. The three condemned men had
little time to ponder their fate.

Henry Amos
Plummer

IN the summer of
1860, eleven years after the famed California gold strike at Sutter's
Creek, an Indian trader named Ed Perce from Walla Walla, Washington, found gold in the sandbar of a creek near what is now Lewiston,
Idaho. News of the strike was slow in spreading, but when it did, the
gold-hungry miners were not slow in coming.

At the time of the discovery, the area was part of the Oregon Territory, which then included the present-day States of Washington, Idaho, Oregon, and Montana and a portion of Wyoming. The Idaho section of the Territory was one of the most rugged and inaccessible areas of the Pacific Northwest. It was shielded from the east by the jagged Bitterroot Mountain Range, a most formidable barrier to cross. To the west was the hostile Blue Mountain Range, and the treacherous Snake River was a moat along the southern barrier. The only practical way to get into the Idaho area was along the old Oregon Trail, which often was impassable during the winter months. It was this inaccessibility that slowed the miners, the gamblers, the outlaws, and the prostitutes in following up the strike by Ed Perce on the banks of Orofino Creek.

Gold, however, still was a powerful lure, and within three years the population of Idaho went from near zero to more than thirty thousand, and most of these were settled around Lewiston and Bannack City. A road was built from the head of Sacramento Valley in California across eastern Oregon to Idaho City, and among the first vehicles to travel it were the Concord stages of the Oregon State Coach Lines, carrying the gold from Idaho to the Wells Fargo vaults in San Francisco.

Among the newcomers to Idaho was a handsome, debonair, soft-spoken man in his late twenties named Henry Amos Plummer. This young man was one of the most enigmatic outlaws of the Old West. He was a murderer, a robber, a bandit, a law-enforcement officer, and an ex-convict. He charmed people of both sexes and easily won their confidence. Some of those he killed had thought themselves to be among his closest friends. Other victims were total strangers.

Plummer's background before he appeared in the West is somewhat of a mystery. Records at San Quentin Penitentiary in California list him as a native of Maine. Historian Thomas J. Dimsdale, in a book written in 1865, said he had been given at least twenty different locations for Plummer's birthplace, including England, but the best guess was Maine. In the files of the Montana Historical Society there is a letter from a Mrs. Z. B. Thibadeau, in which she states that her father knew Plummer in Maine. She says also that her family followed Plummer from Maine to Wisconsin and later on to California. A William Dalton and his family also followed in Plummer's wake, from Maine to Wisconsin to California, and later on to Montana.

Plummer was not a big man. The San Quentin records list him as five feet eight and one half inches tall, with a light complexion and light brown hair. He had moles on the back of his neck and under his left shoulder blade, and three fingers on his left hand were permanently clinched by scar tissue caused by a severe knife wound. Numerous scars on other parts of his body also are listed. In contrast to the custom of the time, he was clean-shaven but for a thin, well-groomed mustache. He was an impeccable dresser.

Another description of Plummer is recorded in a letter written by a William G. Rheem to the Helena (Montana) *Herald* on January 5, 1882: "He was about five feet, eleven inches in height and weighed about one hundred fifty pounds. He was straight, slender, spare and agile. The observer beheld a well cut mouth, indicating decision, firmness and intelligence, but not a line expressive of sensuality; a straight nose and well-shaped chin and cheeks rather narrow and fleshless, still, in their outlines, not unhandsome." Rheem then got carried away. "But," he continued, "one might as well have looked into the eyes of the dead for some token of a human soul as to have sought it in the light gray orbs of Plummer."

The record began to build on Henry Amos Plummer early in 1856 in Nevada City, California. Two men, Jim Webster and Robert Farnesworth, escaped from the city jail one afternoon. Plummer, who only recently had arrived in the community, said that he could recognize the two desperados because he had known them while doing police work in San Francisco. A citizen's posse was formed and gave chase. Meanwhile, Sheriff W. W. Wright and his deputy, David Johnson, were already trailing the two escaped prisoners.

Shortly after nightfall, Plummer became separated from his posse. The leaderless posse halted some miles outside the city as its members debated whether the two escapees were really worth recapturing. They had decided to return when they heard the sound of distant gunfire. Turning about, the citizens raced toward the sound, and a little less than an hour later they came upon the bodies of Wright and Johnson, who had been ambushed beside a large cliff. While there, they once again heard the sound of gunfire in the distance. Once again they gave chase, but this time they found nothing. They returned to Nevada City with the bodies of Wright and Johnson and reported that Plummer also could have been ambushed by the two escaped prisoners.

Plummer, however, rode back into town shortly after noon the next day. He had spotted the two prisoners, he reported, immediately after they had murdered the sheriff and his deputy. He had trailed the two killers for several miles before losing them in the dark.

The two escapees were never caught, but Plummer was feted for his bravery in attempting to capture them single-handed. Two days later, he was sworn in as Nevada City's town marshal. He was twenty-four. For two years, Plummer apparently did an adequate job in preserving the peace in that mining community, and he attracted enough support to run for the California Assembly. He won the nomination, resigned as town marshal, and was narrowly defeated for the state office by his opponent in the general election. After his defeat, he was immediately reappointed town marshal.

Shortly after this, he met a young, pretty, black-haired lass named Marie Katherine Vedder. Marie also was Mrs. John E. Vedder. One account says Marie met Plummer when she sought protection from her raging husband. The Sacramento *Union* reported that she sought out Plummer as a counsel in her suit for divorce against Vedder. The relationship between Marie and Plummer, however, quickly evolved into one of a more personal nature than that of a client and counselor or a citizen and law-enforcement officer. Vedder took the child of the marriage and placed it in the custody of friends who lived outside the community. He continued, however, to live in the same house as Marie until mid-September, when he left Nevada City for a business trip to Sacramento. He returned to Nevada City around eleven P.M. on the night of September 26, 1857.

Nevada City was sufficiently small so that the liaison between Marie Vedder and the town marshal was known to most of its inhabitants. When Vedder paused at the local saloon for a nightcap before going to his home, most of the patrons had a good idea of what the husband would find on his arrival. Consequently, when Vedder left after one drink, a half-dozen patrons of the bar followed him at a discreet distance. To have an affair with a married woman was considered very bad taste in those days of the chivalrous West, and Plummer had lost much of his support.

Vedder entered the house from the rear. He had been inside but a few minutes when the cluster of men gathered outside the small dwelling heard loud voices, a scream, then four shots fired in rapid succession. The back door burst open. Vedder staggered out of the house, spun around, and fell to the ground. A moment later, a window opened in the front of the dwelling and Plummer leaped out, a revolver clutched in his right hand. In the moonlight he saw the cluster of men, most of whom now were pointing guns at him. Slowly he lowered his weapon, then turned it over to one of the citizens.

Vedder was quite dead, killed by four bullets which had entered his back. Plummer was immediately removed as town marshal by the citizens outside the Vedder house and arrested and jailed in the small cell behind his former office. He was indicted for murder by a grand jury on October 15. In a one-day trial, held on December 27, Plummer was found guilty of murder in the second degree. How the second-degree verdict was reached is somewhat of a mystery, as Vedder had been shot in the back. Possibly the jury was influenced by testimony from Marie Vedder that her husband had entered the bedroom with his gun in his hand and that Plummer had fired in self-defense.

Plummer's conviction was appealed to the California Supreme Court, in a process that took approximately a year, and was upheld. The former town marshal was sentenced to ten years in San Quentin Penitentiary. As soon as Plummer entered San Quentin, public sentiment in Nevada City began to turn in his favor. Marie Vedder was blamed as the cause of the whole tragedy, and she was so shunned by the community that she fled to San Francisco. Petitions signed by Nevada City's leading merchants and officials, asking for Plummer's pardon, were sent to the governor. Letters were also sent to the governor from San Quentin officials, asking for Plummer's release because the former town marshal was dying of consumption and should be released from confinement. Plummer served nine months of his sentence before the governor succumbed to the pressure and granted a pardon.

In less than a week after his return to Nevada City, Plummer dramatically demonstrated that the town's sympathy had been misguided. He savagely pistol-whipped a man to death in one of Nevada City's brothels. The citizens were embarrassed by the incident, but no charges were brought against Plummer. There were no witnesses as to the cause of the dispute, and Plummer's offhand explanation of self-defense could not be disproved.

A few weeks later, a lone masked highwayman attempted to hold up a Wells Fargo stage in the Washoe Valley of Nevada. As the bandit moved in on the driver, he shifted his shotgun and, ironically, both barrels fell off. The stage driver immediately whipped his horses into a dead run and escaped. A couple of days later, Plummer brought his shotgun to gunsmith Granville Stuart in Nevada City to have the barrels remounted. The coincidence was too much for local law-enforcement officials. They arrested Plummer and charged him with attempted robbery. The charge was dropped a short time later, however, when the stagecoach driver could not identify Plummer as the bandit.

In less than a month, Plummer again was in trouble. This time, he killed a man named Ryder during a quarrel over two prostitutes in the Nevada City brothel where he earlier had pistol-whipped a man to death. Plummer was arrested and jailed to await grand-jury indictment for the Ryder murder. Before the grand jury convened, however, Plummer escaped. There are two versions of his getaway. One reports that a young woman smuggled into the jail a pair of revolvers and that he left Nevada City with a turnkey as a hostage. The other report states only that he bribed his way out of jail. In either case, Nevada City and the State of California had seen the last of Henry Amos Plummer.

He drifted into Idaho Territory, or what was soon to become Idaho. The reports of his activities during the ensuing months are vague and conflicting, but there he apparently teamed up with Bill Mayfield, an escapee from the state prison in Carson City, Nevada. There was a brief flurry of robberies and holdups, mostly of lone travelers, and descriptions of the bandits matched those of Mayfield and Plummer. The partnership did not last long. The partially decomposed body of a man believed to be Mayfield was found near Walla Walla, Washington. The man had been killed by a bullet fired into the back of his head.

Plummer was next reported heading up a gang of outlaws who ranged from Lewiston through the mining camps of Elk City, Florence, Orofino, and others. When a permanent posse was formed to run him down, the gang was disbanded, and Plummer drifted east with a crony named Charlie Reeves.

In a diary kept by James Stuart is the following entry, made during September, 1862: "On our way to Hell Gate at Beaver Dam Hill, we met two fine looking men. One of them said his name was Henry Plummer, the other was Charles Reeves. They were from Elk City on Clearwater and inquired about the mines at Gold Creek and at Beaverhead. We liked their looks and told them that we were only going down to Hell Gate and would return to Gold Creek in a few days."

Plummer was making no attempt to keep his identity secret, despite the fact that he was wanted for murder back in Nevada City. It is known that he and Reeves went to Gold Creek. On September 21, 1862, the pair, accompanied by two other men known only as Woody and York, departed for the Grasshopper Mining District, where Bannack City was just starting to boom. In Bannack City, Plummer left his companions and teamed up with Jack Cleveland.

In the early fall, Cleveland and Plummer left Bannack City, headed for Fort Benton, from which they apparently intended to take a mackinaw boat down the Missouri to the United States. The Indians were acting up, however—several settlers had been killed— and the two men were unable to make contact with any of the mackinaw boats.

While they were waiting in Fort Benton, Plummer and Cleveland met a J. A. Vail, who ran a government farm on Sun River. Vail was worried about the Indian unrest, and he wanted to hire some protection for his wife, his two children, and his sister-in-law, who were living on the farm with him. Plummer and Cleveland appeared to be ideally suited for such work, and Vail hired them. Although Vail was not overly impressed with Cleveland, he found Plummer a thoroughly witty and charming young man.

So, unfortunately, did Electa Bryan, Vail's young and beautiful sister-in-law. The two bodyguards had been on the farm less than a week before Electa Bryan fell deeply in love with the captivating Plummer. Apparently, Plummer also fell in love with Electa, and they began to seriously talk of marriage. To complicate matters, Cleveland also fell in love with Electa, and Vail and his wife were violently opposed to any romance between Miss Bryan and either of the guards. Vail decided the Indians were a lesser threat than the two men whom he had hired. He fired them, and they left for Bannack City, but not before Plummer had promised his betrothed that he would return for her.

The rupture between the two partners that started over Electa climaxed on the evening of January 14, 1863, in Skinner's Saloon in Bannack City. Both Cleveland and Plummer were drunk, and witnesses agreed that Cleveland pulled his gun first. Cleveland's shot went awry. Plummer then shot his partner twice, knocking him to the floor, then ordered him to get up and shot him twice more.

Cleveland was not killed instantly. He was taken to the cabin of a friend, Henry Crawford, where he lingered on for several hours before he died. Plummer then became antagonistic toward Crawford. He harassed Crawford constantly, apparently convinced that Cleveland had told Crawford about Plummer's past, and demanding to know what Cleveland had said during his last hours of life. Crawford insisted that Cleveland had told him nothing, that Cleveland had remained unconscious until his death, but Plummer refused to believe him. With no provocation, he started arguments with Crawford, but Crawford would not draw his gun.

One night, about two weeks after Cleveland had died, Crawford and Plummer chanced to meet in Skinner's Saloon. In this encounter, unlike their previous ones, Plummer made no attempt to start an argument. Instead, he downed his drink and left the tavern. His departure aroused the suspicion of a man named Baker, who followed Plummer and saw him hide behind a large tree near Crawford's cabin. Baker returned to the saloon and told Crawford that he probably was going to be ambushed on his return home.

Crawford made a large circular detour from the saloon to his cabin, approaching the tree from the opposite direction. Plummer was leaning against the trunk, watching the front of Crawford's cabin. His gun hung loosely in his hand. Crawford took no chances. He took out his own revolver, aimed carefully, and squeezed the trigger. The bullet struck Plummer in his right arm and knocked the revolver from his hand. Crawford then left Plummer to seek his own medical aid and proceeded to his cabin, where he packed up his few personal possessions. He rode out of Bannack City before dawn and disappeared.

With Crawford gone, Plummer once again became the charming and debonair adventurer, friend to all, a strong proponent of law and order. He talked at length with leading citizens of the community about the increasing crime rate and how, if it continued, it could threaten the very existence of Bannack City. When a deputation of citizens approached him and asked him to run for sheriff of the Grasshopper Mining District, he accepted with alacrity. With the support of both the decent citizens and the community's desperados, he was overwhelmingly elected to the top law-enforcement position on May 24, 1863. The following week, he left for Sun River to renew his courtship of the beautiful Electa Bryan.

Electa was overjoyed to see her beloved at the Vail ranch, and because of her infatuation Plummer was given a reluctant welcome by Vail. Another house guest was Francis M. Thompson, an agent of the

St. Louis and Montana Mining Company. Thompson had long been close to Electa, and the Vails implored him to talk her out of the marriage. Thompson had heard of Plummer from other freighters, who had described him as one of the worst of the desperados infesting Bannack City. When Plummer showed up at the Vail ranch, however, Thompson quickly succumbed to Plummer's charm and completely discounted all the stories he had heard. Another friend of the Vails', one Joseph Swift, thought Plummer was "one of the greatest men" he had ever met. With both Thompson and Swift supporting Plummer, the Vails gave in. Electa Bryan and Henry Plummer were married on June 20, and promptly departed for Bannack City.

Gold was discovered in nearby Alder Gulch, and the population began to grow. Plummer began to reorganize the Sheriff's Department. Deputies were discharged for incompetence or cowardice. The number of stagecoach holdups increased. Freight wagons were looted by bandits so regularly that none would depart without armed guards. The lone traveler became virtually a memory, for to travel alone was tantamount to suicide. As the deputies turned in their badges, they were replaced by thugs and cutthroats recruited from Skinner's Saloon. One deputy, Ed Dillingham, refused to quit. In June, Dillingham was in Virginia City, the main camp for the Alder Gulch strike, about seventy miles east of Bannack City. He overheard two of Plummer's recently appointed deputies plotting the murder and robbery of a prospector who was believed to have a large amount of gold hidden in his cabin. Dillingham warned the prospector, then confronted his fellow deputies. They became so incensed over Dillingham's actions that they shot and killed him on the spot.

The two deputies were promptly captured by a group of angry miners, and trial was set for the next day. In preparation for the trial, the miners caroused the night away in the saloons of Virginia City. When the court convened the following day, it is unlikely that there was a sober person in the audience, on the jury, or on the bench.

The trial was brief. "These two men, Deputies Buck Stinson and Jack Lyons, murdered Ed Dillingham last night," the prosecutor said thickly. "Do you find them guilty or not guilty?"

"Guilty," roared the audience, the jury, and the bench.

"Then let's hang the sunsabitches."

The assembly agreed loudly. Two prostitutes suddenly began to wail and weep. The men became nervous and self-conscious. The wailing became louder.

"I reckon they can't be all bad," someone said.

"Yeah, let 'em go," the court said.

Stinson and Lyons won only an eight-month extension of life, before they were hanged by vigilantes.

In Bannack City, Sheriff Plummer erected a three-man gallows as a warning to bandits. At the same time, he recruited more men into his band of outlaws, cutthroats such as Haze Lyon, Whiskey Bill Graves, George Ives, Bill Hunter, Bill Moore, Frank Parrish, and Erastus "Red" Yeager. Most carried the badge of a deputy sheriff. Plummer and his masked deputies attacked stages and freighters, and slaughtered lone travelers for the most trivial sums. When the crime was reported to Sheriff Plummer, he and his deputies would leap onto their horses and race out of town in pursuit of the elusive outlaws.

Shortly after Plummer's marriage to Electa, the Vails moved from Sun River to Bannack City, and Plummer, conscious of his image as a law-and-order figure and prominent citizen, used their home as an entertainment center for other prominent citizens in Bannack City. Guests at some of these soirees included Sidney Edgarton, Chief Justice of the Idaho Territory, a man who soon would be elected Senator and the Territorial Governor. At one of these meetings, the subject of forming a vigilante committee to fight the bandits was raised.

Plummer was opposed. "Law and order must be administered by the duly constituted authorities," he insisted. "Otherwise, the very concept of law and order is destroyed and we have anarchy."

The marriage did not progress well. Three months after the ceremony, Electa Bryan Plummer bade her husband farewell and boarded a stagecoach for a long trip back to the East. Some reports say that she carried a trunk full of Plummer's loot with her, but there is no evidence to support these assertions. She never saw Plummer again and, as near as can be determined, never even wrote him a letter.

The robberies and the murders continued during the summer. Despite the gallows, no desperado was apprehended, and some of the citizens quietly began to question the efficiency of their recently elected sheriff. Then, very quietly, they began to question more than his efficiency. The finger of suspicion was first pointed by Henry Tilden, a distant relative of Chief Justice Edgarton's. Tilden told friends that while he was searching for some strayed cattle he had been held up by a group of masked men. One of the robbers, he said, looked very much like Sheriff Henry Plummer, and sounded very much like him as well. Then Deputy Bill Moore exchanged a watch in settlement of a bar bill. The owner of the watch was in the bar at the time. It had been taken from him some two weeks earlier during a stage robbery.

He appeared to accept Moore's explanation that he had found the watch while giving chase to the stage robbers, but he speculated at length over the incident with friends in Bannack City. Other bar patrons recalled similar incidents, in which deputy sheriffs had traded wallets and other watches or jewelry in payment of bar bills. The robberies and holdups continued, and Plummer and his deputies were unable to capture even one of the outlaws.

The beginning of the end came in December of 1863. There lived in Alder Gulch a young man named Nickolas T'Balt, who worked for two merchants named Burtchy and Clark. T'Balt was a popular young man, well liked by everyone. He had come to Alder Gulch to prospect, but had not done well. Gradually he had sold most of his prospecting paraphernalia. Among the equipment still left was a span of mules, which he kept pastured at a place known as Dempsey's Ranch, below Virginia City. Burtchy and Clark bought T'Balt's mules, paid him in advance, then sent him to Dempsey's Ranch to pick up the animals and bring them to Alder Gulch.

T'Balt did not return. His two employees, not believing the sheriff's suggestion that T'Balt had probably skipped with both the mules and the money, went to Dempsey's Ranch. The mules still were there. T'Balt never had arrived. Burtchy and Clark returned to Alder Gulch to organize a search party.

Meanwhile, a Nevada City, Montana, saloonkeeper, William Palmer, accompanied by his young son, went grouse hunting along Wisconsin Creek near the Dempsey Ranch. He flushed a bird and shot it on the wing, and the bird fell to the ground in a small brushy area. The son ran in to pick up the grouse, then stopped abruptly. The dead bird was lying on the corpse of a young man who had been shot once through the head.

Palmer's first thought was to bring the body to Nevada City for possible identification and burial. He found, however, that he could not handle the body with only the help of his small son. He recalled passing a wickiup, a small, crudely built hut, a short time earlier. He drove his wagon to the wickiup for aid. Inside were five men, all of whom laughed at Palmer's plea for help. Infuriated, the saloon-keeper went back to the brush site, where, after a considerable struggle, he managed to load the body of the dead man into his wagon. The dead man carried no wallet or identification.

He arrived in Nevada City in mid-afternoon. A short time later, a miner who had lived previously in Alder Gulch identified the body as that of Nicholas T'Balt. He was buried that day in Nevada City. The following morning, a still furious William Palmer rode to Alder Gulch, where he told the story of his grisly find and the refusal of help by the five men in the wickiup.

Burtchy and Clark saw no need to disturb the sheriff in Bannack City. This was a problem that could better be handled on a local level. Within an hour, a posse of about twenty-five armed Alder Gulch citizens was cantering toward the small wickiup near Dempsey's Ranch. By the time the posse arrived at the brush-covered hut, the quintet had grown from two to seven. One of the men was known to everyone in the posse: Deputy Sheriff George Ives. Furthermore, many in the posse recalled that Ives had been talking to T'Balt shortly before T'Balt left town, and that Ives had followed T'Balt out of Alder Gulch.

A posse member suggested that all seven men be hanged on the spot. They all obviously were outlaws. "He shot the kid," one of the outlaws, Long John Frank, said, pointing to Ives.

"That means you knew about it, so you are guilty also," Palmer replied.

The remaining five members of the gang feigned surprise over the killing, and the posse apparently believed them, as it bound only Frank and Ives to its horses and headed for Nevada City. The citizens were less sympathetic, however, to a George Hilderman, whom they ran into on their way to town, for they disarmed him, trussed him up with the other prisoners, and tossed the trio into a makeshift jail to await trial in the morning. It has never been made clear why Hilderman was a suspect in T'Balt's murder.

W. F. Sanders, a prominent attorney from Bannack City, and a man who on more than one occasion had been a guest of Plummer's at the Vail home, was in Nevada City when the posse arrived with the prisoners. It was Sanders, along with a prominent Nevada City citizen, Jim Williams, who argued successfully that a legitimate trial was needed more than a lynching. Two judges, Byam of Nevada City and Wilson of the Junction Mining District, were chosen to preside over it.

Sanders was named prosecutor, and the trial was scheduled to start in five days.

Word was sent to Plummer that one of his deputies again was facing a murder charge. He responded by sending several of his deputies to Nevada City to preserve law and order. Bandits and outlaws began drifting into town, and rumors that the accused were to be freed by the outlaws spread through the community. A huge twenty-four-hour guard made up of armed merchants and miners surrounded the rickety jail. Next it was rumored that Plummer had demanded custody of the prisoners. "I believe Plummer's one of them," said Edgar Willar, a Nevada City businessman and Mason. "It's time we formed a vigilante committee."

Miners began arriving by the hundreds in Nevada City to guard against any interference with the trial. Word of the arrests had spread through all of the mining districts in the area, and the miners, tired of being victimized, were seeking revenge. Because there was no building in the community large enough to hold those wishing to see the trial, an "open-air" court was set up outside, despite the freezing weather. The judges' bench consisted of two wagons. The twenty-four-man jury, which was picked in less than a half-hour, sat in wooden chairs donated by residents. A huge log fire was kept burning in the center of the outdoor court. The spectators and jurors also kept warm by slipping into Palmer's saloon for fingers of hot whiskey.

Ives was tried first. He not only was accused of the murder of T'Balt, but was identified by stage drivers, freight drivers, and miners as the man who had either pistol-whipped or shot them during robberies or holdups. Then Long John Frank testified that Ives had shot T'Balt after he had robbed him. The trial was a long one by the standards of the era, lasting most of the day. As dusk approached, Judge Byam turned the case over to the jury. This group deliberated a half-hour before it returned with a "guilty" verdict. A quarter-hour later, Ives was hanged from a beam used to hoist hay into the loft of a Nevada City livery stable. Long John Frank was let go. According to some reports, his freedom was given because he testified against Ives. Other reports say he escaped trial because he cooperated with the vigilante committee that was being formed at Willar's suggestion before Ives's trial. Hilderman was exiled from the Territory and told he would be executed if he ever returned.

Within a week after the trial, the vigilante committee formed in Virginia City numbered about fifty persons. With Long John Frank as their apparent informant, the committee decided its first target would be the five men let loose at the wickiup by the posse that had captured George Ives. According to Frank, one of the men, Alex Carter, had been with Ives when T'Balt was ambushed. Carter and Whiskey Bill Graves had fled to Deer Lodge. A group of twenty-five vigilantes, traveling in twos and threes to avoid suspicion, set out for Deer Lodge to capture and hang the two men.

Several of the small groups of men were overtaken during the long journey by Red Yeager, a man seen often in Bannack City and also seen often with Sheriff Henry Plummer. Yeager was vague about the obvious urgency of his business, but when the vigilantes arrived in Deer Lodge and discovered that their quarry had departed hurriedly a few hours earlier, they had good reason to suspect the cause of Yeager's haste.

Residents of Deer Lodge confirmed their suspicions. The vigilantes found a witness who knew Yeager and had seen him in Deer Lodge a short time earlier with Carter. Other witnesses reported that all three men had departed hurriedly in less than a half-hour after Yeager's arrival. Disappointed and angry, the vigilantes headed back to Virginia City. Their return route took them past Dempsey's Ranch and the wickiup where Palmer had gone for help in removing T'Balt's body.

The wickiup was occupied. A thin trail of smoke twisted upward in the cold, windless sky. The vigilantes quietly surrounded the crude hut and called for everyone to come out. The first man through the door was Red Yeager. With him was Frank Brown, a bartender from Nevada City. They were the only two men in the wi kiup.

Yeager admitted that he had carried the warning to Carter and Graves.

"Who told you to do so?" one of the vigilantes asked.

"The leader," Yeager replied.

"And who is that?"

"The sheriff, Henry Plummer."

Yeager tried to make a deal for his life in the same manner as had Long John. He gave the vigilantes the names of twenty-six other members of the gang led by Henry Plummer, several of whom wore deputy-sheriff badges, but the vigilantes merely noted the names. When Yeager fell silent, they hanged him from the branch of a nearby tree. Then, almost as an afterthought, they hanged Frank Brown.

Leaving the bodies hanging from the tree, the vigilantes then cantered on into Bannack City. They found Plummer in his office along with two of his deputies, both of whom had been named by Yeager as part of the Plummer gang. One of the men was Buck Stinson, the same deputy who had killed Ed Dillingham some months earlier. The other was a Ned Ray.

The vigilantes disarmed the three men and marched them outside to the gallows that Plummer had built as a "warning" to outlaws. The three condemned men had little time to ponder their fate. Three ropes were thrown over the crossbeam of the gallows, and the nooses were dropped over the three men's heads. No boxes were readily available to provide a drop, so the three bodies were lifted to the shoulders of the vigilantes, then thrown into the air. It made their deaths slow and painful. The few witnesses who saw the executions said Ray and Stinson died cursing, while Plummer pleaded for mercy.

Within the next few weeks, the vigilantes lynched twenty-six more men, most of whom were on the list furnished by Yeager. The holdups, the robberies, the beatings, and the murders stopped abruptly. The thugs and bandits who escaped lynching fled the Territory. Bannack City and Virginia City became as docile as a New England village.

A few weeks after Plummer's execution, a new sheriff named Bill Thompson was elected to replace him. Some of his predecessor's personal effects were still in his office, and Thompson went to Vail for Electa's address in order that he might send them to her. She was Plummer's only known survivor. She had married again, this time to a farmer in South Dakota. Thompson sent her the personal effects of her former husband, but he never received an acknowledgment.

*Black Jack and Downing paused long enough in the office to
arm themselves heavily from the arsenal collected by Alvord,
then strode across the street to the livery where they
helped themselves to horses and rode out of town.*

Burt Alvord and
Thomas E. Ketchum

SHERIFF Burt Al-
vord was a lawman who made crime pay. In many ways, he was similar
to his counterpart in Idaho, Sheriff Henry Plummer. Like Plummer,
he had the pleasant, winning manner that is required of most confidence men, but, unlike Plummer, he was not a gunman who was
elected to a law-enforcement position.

Until he ran across Thomas E. Ketchum, Burt Alvord had led an exemplary life. An only child, he came to Arizona with his parents when he was in his early teens, and it is believed that he was brought up on a small ranch near Patagonia. On his twenty-first birthday, he was appointed deputy sheriff. Alvord was a big man. More than six feet tall, he had powerful shoulders, and his favorite way of handling recalcitrant citizens was to knock them to the ground with the back of his hand. A couple of years after he was named deputy sheriff, he ran for office as a full sheriff and was elected. It was his job to keep law and order in the southeast corner of the Territory of Arizona, and he roamed from Willcox on the north to Nogales on the south along the Mexican border as far east as Douglas. He was well liked by all of his constituents, who also were highly impressed by his ability to keep the crime rate down. Then Thomas E. Ketchum appeared in the town of Nogales.

Nogales is two cities in one. The border between the United States and Mexico cuts directly through the city, with the larger portion in Arizona. In the summer months it becomes very hot, and many of the Arizonans for years have adopted the siesta habit of their neighbors across the border, closing down their business and napping during the peak heat of the day.

Before the turn of the century, the habit of the siesta was more pronounced than it is today. The only two places that remained open on the United States side of the border were the general store and the International Bank. The rest of the community dozed during the heat of the day.

About thirty minutes past noon on a day in early August, 1894, three men on horseback entered the city from the east. Two of the men wore high-crown Stetson hats and the conventional garb of the Texas cowboy. The third member of the trio was dressed in black. Except for his white shirt, everything he wore was black: the business jacket, the pants, his shoes, which shone despite a patina of dust, and a flat black hat. His face was covered with heavy black whiskers, and a huge black mustache swept down into his beard.

The three walked their horses slowly to the International Bank, which was housed in a small one-story wooden frame building. There they dismounted, throwing the reins to the ground to keep their well-trained horses from moving. One of the men strolled over to the side of the building and leaned against the wall. His companions entered the bank.

Despite the siesta, there were three customers in the building, along with two tellers, an accountant, and the bank's president, John Dessart. The man in black walked over to the door leading to the office of the president, opened it, and stepped inside. A moment later, he returned to the lobby of the building with a gun pressed to Dessart's head. As his accomplice unsheathed his gun from its holster, the man in black announced that a robbery was in progress, and cautioned against anyone making a foolish move. He spoke softly in a well-modulated tone, which, according to Dessart, was much more frightening than if he had snarled or shouted. There were two vaults in the bank. The larger one was in Dessart's office, and it contained approximately a hundred thousand dollars. The bandits, however, apparently were unaware of its existence. They rifled the tellers' cages and then forced Dessart to open the smaller safe, which was behind the cashier's desk.

Less than ten minutes after they had entered the bank, the two bandits left, joined their companion outside, and cantered across the border into Mexico. They had taken a little more than sixteen thousand dollars from the International Bank.

This was the first known appearance in Arizona of Thomas E. Ketchum, who very quickly picked up the nickname of "Black Jack" because of the clothes he wore, but who personally favored the alias of "Matt Burks." His two companions in the robbery were his brother Sam and a man named Jess Williams.

Tom "Black Jack" Ketchum, alias Matt Burks, and his brother Sam were two of three sons born to a doctor in a central Texas frontier town near the site of Fort Concho. The oldest son, Barry, remained in Texas and also became a doctor. Sam and Tom, however, were surly, ill-tempered, and incorrigible. Tom was more of a problem than Sam. He became a fugitive before he was out of his mid-teens after he burglarized a grocery store and severely beat the unresisting owner. Tom took the proceeds of this robbery and escaped into New Mexico.

A couple of years later, he appeared in a saloon in Richland Springs, Texas. There he became involved in a dispute over a card game, during which he shot and killed a gambler by the name of William Powers. Once again he fled. A posse followed him as far as the Mexican border, where he escaped.

He is believed to have remained in New Mexico as a fugitive for a couple of years. There were several reports that he was engaged in continuous fights, many thefts, and some holdups in the New Mexico territory. If he was, the details of his activities have long been forgotten.

In 1886, when he was twenty years old, he surfaced in El Paso, Texas. There, once again, his ill temper got him into a bar fight. His victim this time was a man named Harry Chase, who had many friends in the saloon. Before Ketchum could slip across either the Mexican or the New Mexican border, he was seized by Chase's friends, bound, and delivered to the local sheriff. He was tried for murder, and sentenced to eight years in the Texas State Penitentiary.

Tom Ketchum was not a docile prisoner, and he served his full term. On his release, he went back to his home town with Jess Williams, a fellow prisoner who was released at the same time. He spent several weeks there before he once again set out for the West, this time accompanied not only by Jess Williams, but by his brother Sam. Several weeks later, they appeared in the town of Silver City, New Mexico. They made a big impression because of their affluent condition and because of the black clothes affected by Ketchum. They were all suspected of being bandits, but there was no record of any holdup in the area to which they could be tied.

The assault by the two Ketchum brothers and Jess Williams on the International Bank in Nogales, however, signaled the start of a crime wave that triggered an uproar in the entire territory of southeastern Arizona. Dessart notified the local deputy sheriff of the holdup, who quickly determined that the bandits had crossed the border into Mexico. He dispatched a messenger to Patagonia, where Burt Alvord was staying, and Alvord arrived in Nogales that night. A posse was formed. They learned from Mexican sources that the bandits had not lingered in Nogales, Mexico. They had ridden straight through town, and when last seen had been heading east. Although he was out of the United States, Burt Alvord and his posse tracked the bandit trio immediately south of the border. The bandits reentered the United States near Naco. The posse was a day behind Ketchum when the bandits paused in Don Luis and forced a rancher's wife to cook them breakfast. North of Don Luis, the posse lost the trail temporarily. It gave the bandits another day's lead. When the posse arrived at El Frieda, it learned that the bandits had been there two days earlier, and that they had taken a steer from a rancher. Alvord had no doubts now that he was on the trail of the bandits, because the rancher described one of them as being dressed entirely in black and somewhat of a "dandy." The rancher also described the black-garbed bandit as being soft in voice. The description fit the robbers of the International Bank in Nogales perfectly.

Alvord called the posse together outside the ranch. His expression was throughtful. "They are two days ahead of us," he told the deputies. "They are probably going through the Pedregosa Mountains, heading for New Mexico. Our progress through the mountains will be extremely slow if we want to escape the risk of ambush, and it is extremely unlikely that we will catch up with them before they slip over the border into New Mexico." Alvord told two of his deputies Bill Stiles and Bob Downing, to remain with him. The rest of the posse he sent back.

The three lawmen continued their pursuit. A couple of days later, shortly before dark, they saw smoke from a fire rising into the sky on the eastern slopes of the Pedregosa Mountains near Chiricahua. The three lawmen tied their horses in a grove and cautiously approached the campfire. Ketchum was stretched out on the ground, his head resting against a log pillow. His black suit hung on a hanger from a tree branch. His two companions squatted around the fire. Three large steaks cooked in a frying pan, and the smell of the meat was tantalizing. Alvord drew his revolver and stepped boldly into the clearing. One of the men by the fire spotted him and reached for his gun, freezing when Alvord shook his head and said, "No." The two other deputies appeared at his side. Tom Ketchum slowly sat up, his eyes fastened on Alvord's badge, which was pinned to his shirt. "You three held up the International Bank in Nogales," Alvord continued. "We have been following you for many days."

The bandits said nothing. The two men slowly turned toward Tom Ketchum.

"You took sixteen thousand dollars in that robbery," Alvord said. "Where is it?"

"We buried it back a way," Ketchum replied.

Alvord motioned to Stiles. "Search them," he ordered.

Stiles expertly frisked the bandits, then checked the saddlebags on their horses. The bandits had approximately two thousand dollars in their possession. Alvord counted it slowly, then, surprisingly, tossed the bundle of notes back into Ketchum's lap. "What is your name?" he asked.

"Matt Burks," Ketchum replied. His voice was very soft, and the words were well articulated. "And may I ask who you are?"

Burt Alvord nodded and gave him his name and added that he was a sheriff in Cochise County. "You made a heap of money in a very short period of time," he said conversationally.

Ketchum nodded slowly and rose to his feet.

"I could have shot you. I could have brought you in," Alvord said.

Ketchum smiled thinly. He glanced at the bills in his hand and then counted out one thousand dollars and passed it back to Alvord. Alvord took the money and pushed it into his pocket. "I think I understand." Ketchum said.

Alvord shrugged. "Good," he replied. "I hope there will be no misunderstanding in the future. I can be found most of the time in Willcox, and I trust that in the future you will call upon me before you bury your loot."

Again Ketchum nodded. "It sounds like a mutually agreeable arrangement."

Alvord and his two deputies returned to Willcox. They told the story of following the bandits into New Mexico and losing them in the Peloncillo Mountains.

The Ketchum brothers and Williams spent a few weeks living it up in Silver City again. Then, in the latter part of October, they once again disappeared from this notorious mining town in New Mexico. On November 3 they sauntered into the small town of San Simon in eastern Arizona. They struck the community post office and got away with more than three thousand dollars. A week later, on November 11, the well-dressed bandit in his black clothes held up Joseph Temple, a cashier for the New Mexico-Arizona Railway at Huachuca. The trio escaped with seventy-two hundred dollars. On both occasions, Ketchum was dressed impeccably in his black business suit and vest and tie, with his shoes shined. His victims and the reward posters began referring to him as "Black Jack."

Alvord, accompanied by Billy Stiles and Bob Downing, again took up the pursuit of "Black Jack." They were out of town but a short time when "Black Jack" held up the post office at Bowie, about twenty miles west of San Simon and only twenty-five miles from Willcox. The trail was still fresh when Alvord arrived in Bowie, and he followed it into the Dos Cabezas Mountains.

Stiles reported later that the second encounter took much same form as the first. This time, however, Alvord explained to the man he knew as Matt Burks that he did not want to have to spend time after every robbery looking for his partner. He expected his partner to come to Willcox and bring his share of the bag there. Alvord also suggested that "Black Jack" conduct his operations farther away from Willcox, but that he come to Willcox early in the spring, when Alvord would outline a project that would make the International Bank robbery in Nogales appear a petty theft by comparison. Stiles did not see how much money Alvord collected from "Black Jack," and he was well appeased with the two hundred that Alvord gave him. Downing presumably got the same amount of money.

"Black Jack" went back to New Mexico and his favorite haunts in Silver City. He had enough money to carry him through the winter, but during this period he lost both his partners. It is not known what happened to Jess Williams. He disappeared in December or January from Silver City, and, as near as can be determined, he was never heard of again. On Christmas Eve of 1894, Sam Ketchum shot and killed a man in a bar. He was arrested, and although he claimed self-defense, he was found guilty of murder. He was sentenced to a twenty-five-year term in the state penitentiary at Santa Fe.

Thus, when the snows melted in early March of 1895, "Black Jack" set out alone for Willcox, Arizona, and his appointment with Sheriff Burt Alvord.

He still affected his black clothes, and he had been in Willcox for two days before it was suggested to Alvord that he might be the notorious "Black Jack" who had operated in the eastern border of the state the previous year. Alvord put the rumors to rest. The newcomer to Willcox was none other than Matt Burks, he said, a highly successful businessman from Texas, and the community could be assured that he was no relation to "Black Jack." The community respected the word of its young sheriff, and Ketchum, alias Burks, played the role of the philanthropic Texan admirably. It was obvious that he was a good friend of Alvord's. He spent much of his time with the sheriff in his office and its one-cell jail. Often they played cards, and the laughter of Downing and Stiles along with Alvord and Ketchum's could be heard by passers-by. Ketchum remained in Willcox for about a week before he rode out of town, saying he was returning to Texas. On the evening of March 12, Downing and Stiles left town, and on the following night the sheriff followed suit. On the night of March 14, the four men met in a small abandoned adobe house near Cochise, where Alvord outlined his plan that would make them all rich.

It is unknown how he got his information, but Alvord knew that the westbound Southern Pacific Express train would be carrying eighty thousand dollars' worth of new gold coins from the Denver Mint on the night of March 16. There was a sharp curve in the tracks near Cochise where the line went through the Dragoon Mountains, just west of dry Lake Willcox. It was Alvord's plan to hold up the train at this spot and take off with the gold. The treasure was to be divided equally among the four men, and the plans called for "Black Jack" to leave the area of southeastern Arizona permanently. Stiles, "Black Jack," and Downing remained in the cabin overnight. Alvord returned to Willcox.

The execution of the audacious robbery worked out perfectly. The train slowed to a crawl at the curve, and "Black Jack" easily leaped onto the train. He climbed up to the roof of the cars, ran along them to the tender, and dropped down into the cab of the locomotive. He pointed his gun at the engineer. "Stop the train, please," he said in his soft voice. The astonished engineer did as he was told. For two or three minutes the three men remained quietly in the cab of the locomotive, the only sound in the still night that of steam blowing out over the huge wheels of the locomotive. The express car was immediately behind the tender. Presently the door of this car slid open, and the armed express messenger leaped out to the ground. "Black Jack" fired one shot, which entered the messenger's shoulder and threw him to the ground. Although he was not mortally wounded, he feigned death and subsequently was ignored by "Black Jack."

The bandit sent the fireman to disconnect the express car from the rest of the train. Passengers on the express pushed their heads out the windows to see what was going on, then prudently withdrew them when "Black Jack" fired a couple of shots down the side of the train.

A few minutes later, the fireman returned to the cab, and the train, pulling the express car, slowly moved on down the tracks. After about a mile, "Black Jack" ordered the train to once again stop, near a point where Stiles and Downing were waiting with some stolen dynamite. As "Black Jack" kept guard over the train crew, Stiles and Downing placed the dynamite in the car. When it exploded, it not only blew the roof off the express car, but shattered the big safe inside it. The gold in the safe was scooped into some leather sacks, and soon thereafter "Black Jack" and the two deputies, carrying the treasure, rode their horses down the narrow mountain trail. A couple of hours later, they trotted onto the hard surface of dry Lake Willcox. The ground was so hard that it left no trace of passers-by. No posse could follow a trail there.

Alvord waited for them on a small island, with fresh horses. "It took a little longer than I had planned," Alvord said. "Get into Willcox as quickly as you can. Go to a saloon and buy some drinks. Be seen. I will take care of things around here."

"Black Jack," Downing, and Stiles galloped away toward Willcox, leaving their tired horses and the eighty thousand dollars in gold in Alvord's possession.

News of the train robbery arrived in Willcox shortly before dawn. Alvord was awakened at his home, and he immediately formed a posse, which went to the scene of the holdup. The train had long since moved on. The posse trailed the fugitives to the dry lake bed, where Alvord threw up his hands, commenting that it would be impossible to track an elephant across that land.

About a week later, the sensation of the holdup had quieted down, and, according to plan, the four men met again in the abandoned adobe house near Cochise. Alvord was very much in charge of the meeting. He gave each of his companions $320 in gold coins, warning them not to spend any of it for a while. "They are newly minted and easily traceable," he said. "Every lawman and every merchant in the West will be on the lookout for these coins. As soon as the heat is off, we will divide up the loot as agreed."

"Black Jack" shook his head. "I don't like it," he said. "I will take my twenty thousand dollars now."

Alvord was not intimidated. "You will take it when the rest of us take it," he said.

"Ya, that's right," Stiles agreed. Downing nodded also.

"Black Jack" sighed and shrugged slightly.

The meeting broke up, and the four men worked their way separately back to Willcox.

About ten days after the holdup, Wells Fargo chief detective John Thacker arrived in Willcox. He met with Alvord. "The gold that was taken belonged to Wells Fargo," he said. "I would welcome your help in the investigation."

Alvord promised his complete cooperation. "We followed their trail to the dry lake bed," he said, "There we lost them."

Thacker nodded.

"It appears that they knew the area fairly well," he commented.

"They are long gone now."

Thacker smiled. "Well, we don't know where to go, so we might as well wait here," he said.

Thacker did not have to wait long. About two weeks after the holdup, Bob Downing went into a saloon in Willcox. He was drunk, and in a generous frame of mind. He bought a round of drinks for the saloon patrons, and paid for it with a couple of ten-dollar gold pieces newly minted by Denver.

The bar was run by a man known as Fat Charlie, and as soon as he saw the money, this public-spirited citizen slipped out of his saloon and ran to Alvord. Alvord was sitting with Thacker in the living room of the latter's boardinghouse when Fat Charlie arrived.

"Bob Downing is spending some new ten-dollar gold pieces at my place," Fat Charlie blurted out in front of Thacker. "They could have come from that train robbery."

Alvord laughed. "You are a good man but a suspicious citizen," Alvord said. Then, turning to Thacker, he commented that Downing was one of his most trusted deputies.

Thacker nodded and grinned. Fat Charlie returned to his saloon.

The next day, Thacker began walking around the town of Willcox. He stopped and introduced himself to many of the merchants and other citizens of the community, and in the ensuing conversations he learned that Downing, Alvord, and Stiles were all good friends as well as stalwart lawmen. He learned also that in recent weeks there had been a fourth man, named Matt Burks, who had become quite friendly with the sheriff and his two deputies. A short time later, Thacker noticed Burks coming out of Fat Charlie's. Burks was dressed entirely in black, in a neatly pressed business suit, a flat black hat, and shiny black shoes, with a black beard and a black mustache that swept down into it. Thacker recalled the unsolved holdup of the International Bank in Nogales and the description of the robber. Thacker sent to San Francisco for Ed Hopkins, a Wells Fargo detective. When Hopkins reached Willcox, he was briefed by the chief detective. Hopkins next went to Stiles's room at the boardinghouse, posing as a tailor's agent. He fitted Stiles for a new business suit. Stiles offered Hopkins some new twenty-dollar gold pieces to pay for the deposit on the suit.

Hopkins threw off his cloak of tailor. He carried the money to the window and looked at it carefully. He then looked sternly at Stiles. "This is some of the money taken in the train robbery the other night, isn't it?" he said. "It is some of the same money that your friend Downing was throwing around Fat Charlie's the other night."

"Who in the hell are you?"

"I am a Wells Fargo agent."

"This money came from my mother. It was a present from my mother."

Hopkins shook his head. "You have been set up to take a fall for this robbery. Downing is setting you up. You will probably be hanged."

"I don't believe it."

"How do you think I got turned on to you, Stiles? Downing is setting you up."

Stiles began to swear softly.

Hopkins dropped his arm across Stiles's shoulders. "I might be able to make a deal. If you will confess to the judge, and turn State's evidence, I might be able to get you off."

Stiles thought the suggestion an admirable one. "Let's go right now," he said.

An incredulous Alvord heard what was happening about a half-hour later. He rushed to the judge's chambers and burst through the door and told the startled Stiles to shut his mouth. He was too late. Thacker and Hopkins arrested Alvord in the judge's chambers, along with Stiles, locked them in the small cell in Alvord's office, then went out and picked up Downing and the stranger known as Matt Burks.

All four suspects were confined in the one-man cell. A deputy named Grundig was appointed temporary sheriff, but Thacker and Hopkins took turns guarding the four robbers during the long night. The following morning, the quartet was brought into court. Stiles stood up, and, with tears streaming from his eyes, he told the judge that he had been forced to make a false confession the day before out of fear for his life, which had been threatened by the Wells Fargo agent, Ed Hopkins. Alvord, "Black Jack," and Downing conveyed their shock over being accused of such a heinous crime. The judge was not impressed. He ordered the four men to jail to stand trial. The single cell was very small, and Billy Stiles was not very popular with his three cellmates. The quartet had been in confinement for less than an hour when an uproar broke out in the cell. Grundig did nothing about it. By the time Thacker and Hopkins arrived on the scene, Billy Stiles had been beaten to the point where he was not expected to live.

Thacker pulled Stiles from the cell and took him to an infirmary operated by a local physician.

Within a couple of days, Stiles had recovered sufficiently to talk. Thacker was very patient. "You are the key to the whole robbery," he told Stiles. "You help us get Alvord, Downing, and Burks and I'll give you a good horse and set you free."

Stiles thought the offer an excellent one. He agreed to appear once again before the judge who had heard his first confession, and once again he related his part in the holdup and implicated his three companions.

"Where is the eighty thousand dollars hidden?" the judge asked.

Stiles shrugged. "I do not know. Alvord hid it. I got three hundred and twenty of it, as did Burks and Downing. We were suppose to get the rest later."

The judge did not think the answer a satisfactory one: neither did Thacker or Hopkins. Stiles was allowed to return to his boarding-house, and Thacker followed him here. "We have to have the money," Thacker said. "As soon as we have the money, we will get you your horse and get you out of here."

"How in the hell am I going to do that?" Stiles asked.

"Get Alvord to tell you what he did with it," Thacker said. "Find out where he buried it."

"And how am I going to do this?"

Thacker had no sense of pity. "We will put you back in the cell." About an hour later, Stiles was returned to the one-cell jail. Thacker delivered him to Grundig at the door, and Grundig took out his key to open the cell. As he did so, Stiles pulled a revolver from his boot, shot Grundig in the shoulder, then opened the cell door to release Alvord, "Black Jack," and Downing. The four men paused long enough in the office to arm themselves heavily from the arsenal collected by Alvord, then strode across the street to the livery stable, where they helped themselves to four horses and rode out of town. Thacker and Hopkins heard about the break about an hour after it happened, and they attempted to organize a posse to set out in pursuit. However, they could get no cooperation from the people of Willcox. Grundig was the only peace officer left in the community, and he was wounded and in the infirmary. The rest of the citizens of Willcox blamed the two Wells Fargo detectives for the entire problem. Not one person in town volunteered to ride after the four bandits.

Alvord and Stiles fled together to Mexico. "Black Jack" preferred his more familar haunts in New Mexico. Downing got as far as Nogales before he was picked up, drunk, by peace officers in that city and returned to Willcox.

As soon as Alvord and Stiles had slipped across the border into Mexico, Alvord had told Stiles to get lost. Stiles did just that. He dropped from sight for more than two years.

Alvord, who spoke fluent Spanish, mixed well in Mexico. He organized a band of approximately a dozen Mexican desperados, which he called the Midnight Marauders, and he ranged along the border from Ciudad Juarez to the California border, robbing saloons and stores, usually at night, on both sides of the line. His men did not hesitate to shoot or knife victims who showed the slightest resistance. They were sought constantly by the Rurales, one of the top police forces of Mexico, and on several occasions they were thought to have been trapped in the mountains of Sonora, but in every instance the band escaped capture. Eventually, Alvord's actions and depredations came to the attention of one of the most powerful Mexican outlaws of the decade, Augustin Chacón. He was one of the most ruthless and cruel bandits ever to roam through the high desert country of Sonora. He was known to have personally murdered at least twenty men by the time he was twenty-one years old. Even the Rurales feared to follow him into his hideout in the Sierra Madre Mountains. How he joined up with Alvord will never be known. There are many stories. One of the most commonly told relates that he had Alvord brought to him and gave him an ultimatum to either join up or be killed. Another version states that Alvord and his Midnight Marauders ran into a band of Chacón's, that there was a shootout and many casualties on both sides. Alvord was brought to see Chacón. The two men found an instant liking for each other and so joined forces.

After the union, the raids against small towns and saloons and stores on the United States side of the border increased, and most of the victims were residents of Arizona. Units of the U.S. Army attempted to track down the bandits, but failed, although on several occasions they chased the Chaconistas deep into Mexico. The harassed citizens turned to the Territorial Government for help, and a few days after this appeal, big, red-faced Burton C. Moosman rode into Nogales. Moosman was head of the Arizona Rangers. Before he was appointed to his current position, the young giant had been general manager of the huge Hash Knife ranch in the Territory, and had achieved a considerable reputation after he broke up one of the worst gangs of cattle rustlers in Western history. He had the reputation of being absolutely fearless and absolutely efficient. The day after he arrived, Alvord led a band of Chaconistas into the small town of Oro Blanco. They robbed the general store and the local saloon, but as they rode out of town one of the saloon patrons put a bullet through Alvord's hand. The day after this raid, the ubiquitous Billy Stiles suddenly reappeared in Mossman's office. "I have a proposition for you," he told Mossman. "I can get you Alvord, but it will cost you five hundred dollars."

Mossman did not quibble. "Payment to be made after he is in custody in Arizona," he said.

Stiles agreed.

Mossman shadowed and trailed Stiles as he left Nogales, crossing into Mexico. He followed him to the foothills of the Sierra Madre Mountains, where Chacón was known to be hiding. But there he lost him. Mossman had no great desire to loiter in Chacón's territory, so he returned to Nogales.

Stiles apparently knew that Alvord was in constant pain from the unhealed gunshot wound in his hand. He may have been a part of the gang, because he was allowed to wander in Chacón's territory unmolested. It is unknown what transpired between Alvord and Stiles while they were in Chacón's camp, but ten days after Stiles had departed Nogales, he and Alvord rode into Willcox, where Alvord surrendered to the sheriff of Cochise County. His wound was healed, and he was brought to trial on train-robbery charges. Stiles, however, refused to testify against him, and Alvord was found guilty only of obstructing the United States mail. Thacker and Hopkins were present at the trial, and they prevailed on the judge to make a proposition to Alvord that if he returned the eighty thousand dollars in gold he would be set free. Alvord merely smiled and said nothing when the proposition was made to him. The judge then sentenced him to ten years' hard labor in the Yuma Territorial Prison, the most desolate and fearsome penitentiary of the West. Burt Alvord served seven years in this infamous prison. He was set free three days ahead of his scheduled time, thus thwarting some Mexican peace officers who were en route to extradite him to their country to face trial for his crimes there.

Thomas Ketchum, alias "Black Jack," alias Matt Burks, apparently had been highly impressed by the potential for profit in train robbery. Shortly after he returned to New Mexico, he held up a train near Albuquerque, was caught, and served a term in the Santa Fe Penitentiary, coincidental with Alvord's in Yuma. He was released at approximately the same time, and he returned to Arizona and settled down in the small town of Payson, in the central part of the state, under the name of Charles Bishop. He had lived there for approximately six months when he journeyed to Camp Verde and held up the Sutless Store. During this robbery he killed two men, Clifton Wingfield and Mac Rogers, and seriously wounded another person known only as Captain Boyd. A posse was formed, but "Black Jack" slipped back into New Mexico and escaped.

A few months later, he was back in Arizona, this time in the northeastern section. He heard rumors that a Colorado and Southern train carried large amounts of gold, and again he decided to try his hand at train robbery. This time he worked by himself. He boarded the train when it slowed for a curve in the mountainous section of the state, once again climbing over the train's tender into the cab and stopping the locomotive. He bound the engineer and fireman and returned to the express car, where he disarmed the messenger and bound him also. He had not, however, disconnected the express car from the rest of the train, and he was in the act of planting dynamite near the safe in the express car when Conductor Frank Harrington pushed open the door to see what was wrong. "Black Jack" saw him and fired a shot at him, which missed. Harrington raised his shotgun and fired at "Black Jack."

The outlaw was found wandering around the area the next day, out of his head and almost minus one arm. Eventually his arm had to be amputated.

Ketchum was brought to trial for the murder of Rogers and Wingfield in Camp Verde, and sentenced to be hanged. He seemed completely disinterested in his fate, but when he mounted the scaffold for his execution, he was dressed in his favorite black suit and black hat and shiny black shoes. At Ketchum's request, a banjo player and a violin player performed at the foot of the scaffold.

Bob Downing spent some years in the Yuma Territorial Prison, but information about the charges for his conviction is vague. On his release, he returned to Willcox, where he was eventually shot and killed during a gun altercation outside a saloon. Stiles moved to Nevada, where he got a job as a deputy sheriff. He was killed some time later while attempting to arrest a town drunk. Burt Alvord disappeared for a few months after his release from the Territorial prison. Then he reappeared in Willcox, where he bought a bottle of whiskey and paid for it with a new ten-dollar gold piece. He purchased a horse and paid for it with two new twenty-dollar gold pieces. Then he disappeared.

Shortly after the turn of the century, the doctor who had healed his hand in Willcox received a letter from Alvord, mailed from Panama. In it was a picture of Alvord and a beautiful Spanish girl standing in front of a magnificent mansion. Mossman sent inquiries to the Panama police. Yes, Senor Burt Alvord did live there. He was one of the city's more affluent citizens.

He died in Panama in 1923.

At the price of gold more than a century later, the $60,000 worth of gold stolen in the last robbery at McLaughlin's way station should be worth at least a quarter million dollars today.

John and Jim Reynolds

THE Reynolds gang operated principally throughout the Colorado area, and it probably would have made no impact upon history if it had not been for the manner in which the gang was broken up and for the tale of buried treasure it left behind. The nucleus of the band was formed by four men from San Antonio, Texas: the Reynolds brothers, John and Jim, Owen Singleterry, Charles Harrison, and another Texan from El Paso, known as Cap McKee. They apparently were drawn together in Denver by their Texas accents and garb.

The quintet is believed responsible for a few holdups and robberies around Denver in the summer of 1862. Singleterry had lost the index and little fingers of his right hand in a gunfight in San Antonio. He was the most notorious badman of the band, and had been involved in at least two gun frays in Denver before the arrival of the rest of the Texans. In early September of 1862, five men held up a stage on the outskirts of Denver. Although the men were masked, the driver pointed the finger of suspicion at Singleterry when he described one of the bandits as having but three fingers on his right hand. Soon after the holdup, a couple of deputy sheriffs ran Singleterry down in a Denver tavern. Apparently he was not arrested, but he was made sufficiently nervous so that he left the city along with his four companions.

According to Henry Sinclair Drago, the gang surfaced in the South Park region of Colorado, where they drifted from one mining camp to another. They engaged in no mining, no prospecting, yet they rode fine horses and spent money lavishly in saloons. This, coupled with the sudden sharp rise in the number of stage holdups and ambush robberies of travelers, again aroused public suspicion that the affluent Texans were the masked bandits plaguing the community.

A few miles outside of Fairplay, Colorado, was a stage way station known as McLaughlin's. On a brisk and chilly day in the late fall, the five Texans seized the way station, terrorized McLaughlin and his wife, and emptied the till. When the stage arrived about an hour later, the gang broke open its strongbox and looted it, stripped the passengers of their valuables, then departed with the mail.

The citizens of Fairplay were irate over this latest outrage. A posse was formed. Witnesses and victims of the robbers said the gang had ridden off in a northerly direction. The posse gave chase, but could find no trace of the highwaymen. The following morning, the members of the posse returned to Fairplay, arriving there about noon. Some members of the posse had gone home, and about twenty were sitting in a tavern discussing the problem when a rancher named Albert Guiraud, who lived five miles south of Fairplay, burst into the tavern.

The five bandits, he reported excitedly, were hiding on his ranch and had forced his wife to make them dinner. The twenty armed men raced to the ranch. The five bandits—Jim and John Reynolds, Singleterry, Harrison, and McKee—were still clustered around the dinner table in the ranch house, incoherently drunk on liquor they had taken with them from the way station. They were disarmed before they realized they had been discovered.

The bandits were taken back to Fairplay, where they spent the night under guard and tied to a hitching rail in front of the tavern. The following day, they were tossed, still bound, into the back of a buckboard and driven to Denver. There they were turned over to the custody of the sheriff. They spent the first night in the Denver jail quietly. On the morning following the second night, when the turnkey arrived at their cell with breakfast, he found the door unlocked. His prisoners had vanished.

The accounts of the escape vary. One report states that the gang stole horses from various saloons after they broke out of the jail and that they were trailed to an area east of old Fort Wise before the chase was abandoned. Another report indicates that they prevailed upon the Confederate sympathies of the jailer and that he not only let them out but secured them mounts. Still another account indicates that the bandits simply bribed the night jailer into letting them go with a tale of buried treasure.

It has been established, however, that the Reynolds brothers and their three companions worked their way successfully back to Texas. If they engaged in any banditry along the way or after their arrival, they certainly were not suspected of it. The nation was locked in its Civil War at the time, and, as was to be expected, the Reynolds brothers supported the Confederate States, as did most Texans. According to Jim Reynolds, shortly after his return to Texas he called on General Henry McCullough, the commanding officer of the Confederate Army in Texas. He proposed to McCullough that the Reynolds brothers head up a guerilla force that would penetrate Colorado and raid the U.S. Mint in Denver. The task force could bring back to the Confederacy much-needed gold and silver.

Reports differ on whether McCullough bought the idea. In one version, McCullough furnished the Reynolds gang with twenty-five soldiers and dispatched them to Colorado. Another report states that the five bandits headed back for Colorado on their own and that they increased the size of their gang to thirty while passing through Las

Vegas, New Mexico, at that time a gathering spot for brigands and cutthroats. In either case, the band gave itself quasi-military status. Jim Reynolds was very much in charge, and he called himself a colonel. Next in command was John Reynolds, with the rank of major, and Singleterry, Harris, and McKee were captains.

According to Drago, the band made a highly successful raid only a few miles from Las Vegas when it struck a convoy traveling to Santa Fe from Chihuahua and escaped into the rugged Sangre de Cristo Mountains with more than sixty thousand dollars' worth of minted gold. With this amount of loot in their possession, the patriotism of the Confederate guerillas diminished substantially. Although Reynolds claimed he wanted to bury the gold for pickup on their return to Texas, the other members of the band demanded that the loot be divided at once. The booty was divided, and the guerillas disbanded. Among those departing were Captains Harrison and McKee. Eight of the self-styled guerillas moved north into Colorado. These were the Reynolds brothers, Singleterry, John Andrews, Jack Robinson, John Bobbitt or Babbit, Jack Stowe, and Tom Holliman. Drago says these men pooled their share of the booty taken in the raid and buried it near Spanish Peaks. It apparently has never been found. (Drago also puts another man in the invading force: Thomas Knight.)

The bandits, or guerillas, crossed into Colorado via Raton Pass without attracting any undue attention, and settled down in the mountainous South Park Region, where they had been successful on their earlier raids. They built a hideout on a high flat mesa amid a grove of aspens. A stone wall about four feet high was built around the camp. A narrow ravine led up to the mesa, which provided for a good defense if needed, but the location of the camp could be seen for many miles.

As soon as the camp was completed, the Reynolds brothers once again began preying on stages, small stores, and miners in the area. It is reasonable to assume that the victims did not at first connect the new flurry of holdups with the same gang captured some months earlier. William Spacer provided the first clue that the new gang of desperados was indeed the Reynolds gang. Spacer was a businessman from Denver, and he was casually held up by four men while en route to Fairplay. He noticed that one of the bandits had but three fingers on his right hand, and when he reported this to the sheriff in Fairplay, that lawman immediately recalled the deformed hand of Owen Singleterry.

The inevitable posse was formed and the search began, but the hideout proved satisfactory. For the next few months, the Reynolds gang roamed all over that region of Colorado. After each holdup, a posse would give chase. On some occasions, three or four separate posses would be on the trail, running into and, on one occasion, shooting at one another, but the Reynolds gang always was successful in getting back to the camp undetected.

There were many stories circulating throughout the area. One held that the posses were less than eager for a confrontation with the Reynolds gang and that when the gang fled to the east, the posses went west. Another contended that the bandits, who still masqueraded as guerillas, were being protected by ranchers living in the rural areas who were sympathetic to the Confederate cause.

The average yield per holdup was low, often not exceeding two or three hundred dollars, and it is unlikely that any of the bandits used this as a payoff throughout the countryside for their personal protection. Additionally, many of their victims were local residents.

Their main goal was to assault the U.S. Mint in Denver, where the gang estimated millions of dollars' worth of gold and silver was cached. Much of it, they thought, had been brought from the East for safety, to prevent it from falling into Confederate hands.

Early in September of 1864, Jim Reynolds and Owen Singleterry left the band and went to Denver to look over the situation. They spent about one week in the city, and apparently they decided that the Mint could be ripped off. Both bandits were flush, and they lived high. According to one report, Reynolds and Singleterry became drunk one night in a Larrimar Street saloon and let a few remarks slip about their future plans for the United States Mint. This information soon came to the attention of Denver Police Captain Hugh Maynard, who became very interested when he learned that one of the drunks was short two fingers on his right hand. Maynard sent out a squad to search the city for the two men, but they had disappeared. The captain then alerted the Mint, where officials promptly doubled the size of the guard.

Meanwhile, Reynolds and Singleterry had returned to the hideout, where they remained quietly for approximately two weeks. Then, early one morning, the band struck out for the capital city.

During the early part of their journey, the bandits avoided the trails, working their way slowly through rough ground. As the day progressed, however, they became more careless, and by late afternoon they cantered openly along one of the main trails to Denver. Shortly before dusk they came upon a wayside inn, and it was a refreshing sight. The men were hot and thirsty and hungry. They decided to bed down there for the night. A few drinks before dinner loosened them up sufficiently to discuss some of the minor details of the raid on the United States Mint. A young man named Lloyd eavesdropped on the conversation for a while, then drifted from the saloon, saddled his horse, and rode through the night to Denver. Early on the following morning, he was routed to Captain Maynard.

Maynard was elated. He immediately swore in a posse and left the city to meet the bandits. The Reynolds gang had gone to bed late and had risen late. Most of the members were slightly hung over. Shortly after noon, the Maynard posse and the bandits collided head on in the middle of the trail. Apparently both sides were surprised. Maynard had expected to confront the bandits at the Wayside Inn, and the gang had had no idea that it would bump into a posse. The shootout between the two opposing forces was brief and lethal. Two members of the posse were killed. Three members of the Reynolds gang were wounded, including Owen Singleterry, but all of the gang were able to scatter in the heavy timber. Captain Maynard and his men scoured the area for more than two days, but by that time all the gang had regrouped in the hideout, and the veteran Denver police officer was forced to give up the search.

While the wounded healed, some members of the gang spread out to undertake small robberies for the cash needed to operate. Jack Stowe and Tom Holliman crossed over the divide to Alma and Breckinridge, where they carried out a couple of profitable stagecoach holdups. Generally, however, the pickings were lean. Shippers were not sending valuables by stage because of the Reynolds gang, and single travelers carried a minimum amount of cash. Money and supplies were becoming critically short, and Holliman and Stowe once again ventured out from their hideout. This time, apparently by chance, they wound up in Fairplay. They paused in a saloon and, instead of talking, for a change, they listened. Because of the activity of the Reynolds gang, gold had been piling up in Fairplay. The dealers who purchased it from local prospectors and miners were reluctant to ship it to Denver for fear that it would be hijacked by the

Reynolds brothers. As a result, there was more than sixty thousand dollars in gold stored in the safe of the Spottswood Stage Lines in Fairplay.

"I heard the Reynolds gang was broken up by Denver police more than a month ago," Stowe volunteered.

A clerk for the stage company was in the saloon. "It seems to be that way," he said. "If there has been no action from the gang by the middle of next week, they are going to make the shipment Thursday."

The previous sixty-thousand-dollar haul netted by the gang in New Mexico had been divided equally among thirty men. This would be an infinitely greater haul, reasoned the Reynolds brothers, because it would need be divided only among eight persons. The Reynolds brothers decided to make their play at McLaughlin's Station. This was the same way station they had held up earlier, from which they had taken the whiskey which led to their capture.

On the following Thursday, about two hours before the stage was due, the gang once again seized McLaughlin's Station. The bandits tied up six patrons inside the inn, broke open the whiskey, and ordered the cook to prepare a meal for them. They had not finished their leisurely repast when the stage pulled into McLaughlin's. The gang almost missed its target.

The stage driver, one Abe Williams, became suspicious when he saw so many horses tethered to the hitching rail with no sign of any men around. He had started to climb back up on the stage when Jim Reynolds glanced out the dining-room window and for the first time noticed that the stage had arrived. Reynolds and Singleterry raced toward the door of the hostelry and burst outside just as Williams picked up the reins of the stage. William McLellan, one of the stage owners, was also "riding up on the box," and when the two bandits came through the door, he reached for his shotgun, then decided against it. Williams dropped the reins, and McLellan kicked his shotgun to the ground.

The remainder of the gang stumbled outside. The strongbox was tossed down and broken open. The passengers on the stage were ordered inside the way station, where they were relieved of their cash and jewelry. A short time later, the Reynolds gang rode away with sixty thousand dollars' worth of gold, four hundred dollars in cash, and a few bottles of whiskey from McLaughlin's bar. According to Drago, the gang did not travel very far, only to Kenosha Pass, a few miles distant, where they spent the night at another inn, Omaha House.

McLaughlin had many friends. A few hours after the robbery, a small posse of these friends was chasing after the outlaws, but was unable to make contact. The following noon, Captain Maynard set out from Denver with an armed posse of thirty men to pick up the trail. At about the same time, another heavily armed posse, organized by Jack Sparks in Fairplay and Swan River, also began trailing the outlaws.

Reynolds and his companions left Omaha House early in the day after the robbery, taking a circuitous route back to their hideout. They did not hurry, apparently believing that no organized pursuit was in progress. However, late in the afternoon, Stowe spotted the Sparks posse riding along a trail that cut them off from their head-quarters. The bandits were not seen as they backtracked away from the hunters. As night approached, the gang worked its way up a canyon (generally believed to have been Handcart Gulch) and made camp, burying the gold taken in the robbery at McLaughlin's way station somewhere nearby.

They remained in Handcart Gulch for two or three days, confi-dent that they could not be found and that soon the posses would give up the chase. Their assumption was accurate in one respect and inaccurate in another. The Maynard posse returned to Denver on the second day. The posse led by Sparks also had given up, and was returning to Swan River. That night, this posse cut through Handcart Gulch, and was preparing to make camp when its members saw smoke from another fire. At first Sparks thought he had run across the Maynard posse, but he was a cautious man. He carefully scouted the distant campfire on foot, and was elated to discover that he had stumbled across the outlaws. Warily, he rejoined his men and ordered them to surround the bandits' camp.

Before the encirclement could be completed, however, one of the deputies accidentally discharged his rifle. The outlaws raced for their horses. Sparks fired at one of the fleeing outlaws in the dimming light, and thought he saw his quarry race away. The posse, all now on foot, made no attempt to give chase at this moment.

Cautiously, the members of the posse entered the camp. The gang had left behind rifles, food, blankets, and cooking utensils, but there was no sign of the McLaughlin loot. The posse members went back for their horses and occupied the camp abandoned by the outlaws. Guards that were posted saw no signs of any attempt by the Reynolds gang to recover its possessions. In the morning, however, one of the posse members did find the body of one of the bandits, Owen Singleterry. It was lying on the ground less than a half mile from the camp.

One of the members of the posse was Dr. George Cooper, of Alma. The doctor severed Singleterry's head from his body and brought it back to Alma, where it was displayed in a large glass jug of saline solution at a local saloon for several years.

The Reynolds gang permanantly scattered that night. John Reynolds, Stowe, and Andrews slipped successfully through the mountains into New Mexico. The first member of the gang to be captured was Tom Holliman. Traveling alone, he made his way to the home of a girlfriend in Canon City. After he fell asleep, exhausted, she notified a local sheriff, who took him into custody. He was taken to Fairplay and jailed.

Jim Reynolds and the remaining members of the band tried for several days to get back to their hideout, but on each occasion they were cut off by the Sparks posse. Whether Sparks had any idea of the general location of the hideout is unknown, but members of the posse always materialized when the bandits neared their sanctuary. Finally, in desperation, they turned toward Fairplay. A few miles from the town, they forced their way into a ranch house, held the family hostage, and made the women cook for them. Then, for two days, they took turns sleeping and standing guard. Despite their precautions, however, a small boy in the family slipped away. When his absence was noticed, the bandits hurriedly saddled up and fled, not even taking the time to load up with some provisions.

Reynolds was correct in his assumption that the boy had gone to Fairplay to tell of his family's predicament. The citizens there assumed correctly that the men were part of the Reynolds gang. A new posse was organized, this one containing almost one hundred men, and the chase was on again. For some unknown reason, the prisoner Tom Holliman was forced to ride with the posse, commanded by a man named Shoup. Most of the Sparks posse still was in the field.

The pursuit lasted for four days, until the Shoup posse caught up with the four exhausted outlaws about thirty miles east of Canon City. Jim Reynolds and his three companions surrendered without a fight and, along with Holliman, were taken to Denver and lodged in the city jail. This time, a twenty-four-hour guard was placed over the outlaws.

Shoup had been away from the jail but a half-hour when he heard reports that his captives were rebel guerillas and that they were being held in the city jail. There was a strong group of Southern sympathizers in Denver, and Shoup began to wonder if some of these rebel supporters might not raid the jail and free Reynolds and his men in the belief that they really were Confederate soldiers. He took his fears to the sheriff, who quickly devised a political solution to his problem.

He declared that his prisoners were indeed Confederate guerillas, and he immediately turned them over to the military garrison in Denver. The military made a similar assumption, and promptly charged the five men with conspiracy in an attempt to overthrow the United States Government. The trial was held within two days of their arrival in Denver. It was conducted secretly. The records have never been made public. Reynolds and his four followers were found guilty and sentenced to be hanged.

As soon as this became known, the military commanding officer announced that the five men would be taken to Fort Leavenworth in Kansas, where they would be held pending a review of their sentence.

On the following day, a unit of the Third Colorado Cavalry, under the command of Captain Theodore G. Cree, took custody of Jim Reynolds and his four companions and marched out of Denver, ostensibly for the long trip to Fort Leavenworth. Cree and his men returned to Denver the next day. The Confederate soldiers, they reported, had all been shot while attempting to escape while passing through the ghost town of Russellville.

About a week later, a well-known Indian scout named Dick Wooten rode through the abandoned mining town of Russellville. Lashed hand and foot to several trees were the bodies of the five outlaws.

At first Captain Cree denied the mass murders. Then he changed his story and said that he had only been carrying out orders, like any good soldier. Cree's contention apparently was accepted by the military. He was promoted and transferred to an undisclosed post in the East. The identity of the officer who gave Cree his orders has never been disclosed.

There are many stories about the ultimate fate of John Reynolds, John Andrews, and Jack Stowe. One account states that Andrews died of wounds received in the Handcart Gulch attack, another that he was shot while holding up a bank in Texas. Stowe reportedly died in a saloon shootout in Texas. There are some reports that John Reynolds returned to Colorado and was shot to death while horse stealing or cattle rustling.

Of more interest to the thousands of treasure seekers throughout the West is what happened to the sixty thousand dollars' worth of gold stolen in the last robbery at McLaughlin's way station. At the price of gold now, more than a century later, the treasure should be worth at least a quarter of a million dollars. If there was indeed that much gold taken from the stage, then it should be somewhere around Handcart Gulch.

*The Nicaraguans then became tired of the same old game and
ended it by standing Walker up against the wall
and filling him with bullets.*

William Walker and Antonio Melendrez

WILLIAM WALKER
referred to himself as a president and a general. He was a bandit, and
he was executed.

Antonio Melendrez considered himself a *bandido,* yet because of
William Walker, his crimes were overlooked. He was made a general
in the Mexican Army, and he lived to a ripe old age.

115

Melendrez operated from La Grulla Ranch outside Ensenada from the late 1840s to the late 1860s. He led what was probably one of the most successful bandit gangs to prey along the western section of the North American hemisphere.

Melendrez had a band that ranged between seventy-five and one hundred men. Until 1853, his victims were the usual lone traveler, the occasional stage, or a store. Sometimes he slipped across the United States border east of San Diego to steal horses and cattle from the rich gringos, which he would drive back to La Grulla Ranch. On one occasion, Melendrez and his men rode deep into the United States in the ranch country east of San Diego. They stole approximately fifty horses from more than a dozen ranchers before they cantered back to the Mexican border. The irate ranchers formed a posse and gave chase. Near what is now Tecate, Mexico, the members of the posse corraled their mounts in a small grove and then made camp on the banks of the Tia Juana River. When they woke in the morning, all the horses were gone. Melendrez had slipped into the grove during the night and silently made off with their mounts.

Unlike other bandits, Melendrez maintained a loose cover, that of a successful ranch operator. The army-police detachment in Ensenada had a very small garrison, and it was no match for the well-organized Melendrez. Thus, Melendrez was accepted for what he was not: a successful and prominent rancher who kept approximately one hundred vaqueros on his payroll. The army-police left Melendrez alone, and Melendrez left the army alone. It was a practical understanding.

Melendrez attacked most of his victims to the north, near Tia Juana and Mexicali. On one occasion he raided some settlements just south of Fort Yuma in the United States. The U.S. Army patrol went after him and was ambushed; three soldiers were killed. Melendrez, however, was not a bloodthirsty bandit like Vasquez. He killed only those who resisted him or threatened to capture him.

He was a tall man. Legend says he was half Mexican and half Yaqui Indian. He had long black hair, which he wore braided down his back under the hat of a vaquero. He lived in his large house at La Grulla with three women. Some stories say he considered all three his wives. Other versions say that only one of the women was his wife; the other two were sisters of his wife.

There is no known record of where he was born. He came into being as a bandit operating near Ensenada in Baja. He did not allow his band to shoot up Ensenada. When a Melendrez bandit felt the urge for rest and recreation, he was sent to Mexicali or Tia Juana, and if he got into trouble there, Melendrez would either bribe a few people or raid the jail to get his vaquero back.

It was after one such raid on the Tia Juana jail, in which a guard was killed, that authorities in Mexico City began showing the first signs of irritation. A letter was sent to the military commander in Ensenada, Colonel Negrete, suggesting that he take all steps necessary to break up the *bandidos* known to be flourishing in Baja. Negrete promptly asked for more men, arms, and money in order to undertake the project. The letter was filed when it reached the nation's capitol.

A few months after that, Melendrez raided a bank in Mexicali. The amount of his loot is unknown, but the bank was owned in part by a businessman in Mexico City with strong connections with the Church hierarchy. The Church complained to the government, and another letter was sent to Colonel Negrete, who replied to it in the same manner as he had the first. Once again, the army in Mexico City filed the reply without comment. It was about this time that William Walker began to surface some six hundred miles to the north in San Francisco.

The late Harry Hopkins once said that anything could be sold to the American people so long as it contained the word "freedom." As a nation, we are peculiarly susceptible to semantic inanities. A few years ago, a California politician made a thirty-minute speech to a large crowd of cheering supporters in which he developed the thesis that freedom from poverty programs was a dire threat to the free enterprise system. A Los Angeles politician, determined that Southern Californians be given freedom from obscenity, has fought a continuing battle against art exhibits and nude sunbathing.

A little more than a century ago, "freedom" was not so popular. A large segment of the United States had fought a bitter war for freedom of the states, and lost, and proponents of freedom were generally considered subversives. Successful businessmen saw no stigma attached to listing their occupation as "capitalist," and those who opposed "manifest destiny" were treated in the same manner as those who object to free enterprise are today.

William Walker, who eventually was to meet his death before a Nicaragua firing squad, was one of the most avid exponents of manifest destiny, and he used it as a cloak to cover his plundering of Mexico and Central America. Much has been written about his freebooting activities in Central America, but little has been reported on his activities throughout Baja. In contrast with Melendrez, a great deal is known about William Walker. He was a man of slight build, with delicate facial features and a good educational background. He had studied both law and journalism successfully in Pennsylvania, Paris, Gottingen, and Heidelberg. After his education in Europe, he returned to the United States, where he was employed as a reporter by a newspaper in New Orleans named the *Crescent.*

The newspaper folded some time later, and Walker drifted west. For a while he worked as a newspaperman in San Francisco; then he moved on to Marysville, where he opened a law practice, taking in with him a close friend named Henry Watkins. It was there, with Watkins, Walker decided that it was his manifest destiny to set up an independent state in Mexico which would be known as the Republic of Sonora and Lower California. In 1853, posing as newspapermen, Walker and Watkins took a leisurely trip to Mexico, going as far south as Guaymas in Sonora. It was as they had anticipated: Conditions were deplorable. Yaqui Indian violence posed a constant threat to innocent women and children. The Mexican Government was doing nothing to combat this unwarranted aggression by the Yaquis; doing nothing to give these democratic, peace-loving people the protection they deserved. Even the security of the United States was threatened by these warlike savages, who, growing bolder every day, soon might sweep across the border and wreak untold horrors upon innocent American women and children. Surely, here was a case of manifest destiny in its finest manifestation. Walker and Watkins headed back toward California, every day becoming more dismayed at the intolerable situation. Even in Tia Juana, just across the border from San Diego, the population lived in constant terror of the marauding bandit gang under the command of Antonio Melendrez. Obviously, they argued, something had to be done.

The two men returned to San Francisco. Their first act was to float a bond issue to raise money for the treasury of the newly formed Republic of Sonora and Lower California. Walker was the president. Watkins was the vice-president. A recruiting office was opened. They had no trouble selling their bonds or raising an army. A large ship named the *Arrow* was purchased to carry Walker and liberation forces to the new nation. Their first objective was the seizure of Baja. Before the expedition could sail, however, the *Arrow* was confiscated by the United States Army under the orders of President Fillmore. The armed men whom Walker and Watkins had recruited were furious. The seizure was considered an outrage in San Francisco, an unwarranted intrusion into the orderly progress of manifest destiny. Many who cared nothing about Walker's project were upset over this arrogant interference on the part of Fillmore. Walker never did recover the *Arrow*, but within two weeks he had raised enough money from sympathizers to acquire a larger ship, called the *Caroline,* all of which apparently escaped Fillmore's attention. Walker sailed unmolested with his army of bandits through the Golden Gate on September 30, 1853. He had forty-six men in his gang, plus the crew of the ship.

His first invasion was at La Paz in Baja, near the tip of the seven-hundred-fifty-mile-long peninsula. When he dropped anchor in the harbor, small boats put out from shore to ferry the bandits to the land. The merchants, as usual, were delighted to see a ship in port. The city lay down before the invaders like a trollop. Walker and his band strolled over to the governor's palace, kidnapped that executive, and took him and a box of state documents back to the *Caroline.* The Mexican flag was lowered and replaced by a two-stripe banner, which Walker said represented his new republic.

Walker then stood on the steps of the governor's piazza and officially proclaimed himself the president of the new nation. A few curious residents mingled with the army to hear the proclamation as beggers, peddlers, and pimps hocked their wares to the assemblage. The new state, Walker told his bandits, would recognize religious toleration and general protection, and the laws would be based on the Louisiana code.

For three days there was a fiesta. The army spent its money in the local cantinas and brothels and then retired to the barracks to await the next splurge on the following payday. Walker, however, had also begun running out of money. He began buying his supplies with money drawn on the national treasury of the Republic of Sonora and Lower California. His welcome immediately wore out in La Paz. Mexican pesos and Yankee dollars were welcome tender, but paper Sonoran dollars had no value at all to the citizens of that community.

The Mexican Army in La Paz consisted of one man, Lieutenant Manuel Pineada, who had been left alone by Walker's conquering bandits because no one knew who he was. When the spending spree was over and the invaders attempted to buy goods with spurious money, Pineada met with some of the merchants, and a decision was reached that the time had come for their guests to depart. There was a problem with the governor, who was still a prisoner on the ship, but the consensus was that the governor was only a politician and could easily be replaced. A counterattack was launched against Walker's bandits. Lieutenant Pineada did not want anyone to be hurt seriously, so his attack, led by himself in command of twelve volunteers, consisted of a barrage of sticks and stones against a six-man detail that was returning to the ship with supplies that had been paid for with Sonoran money.

Walker, who referred to his takeover of the community as a military maneuver, became incensed over this sudden terrorist activity. He immediately put some thirty armed men ashore, and Lieutenant Pineada prudently withdrew his volunteer army. He obviously was becoming upset over the state of affairs, however, and he dispatched a message to the Mexican Army detachment station at a camp some one hundred kilometers to the north.

Walker, still wearing his general's hat and ribbons, interpreted Pineada's withdrawal as a signal victory for his troops. He sent word of the encounter to San Francisco, where Watkins held a press conference, in which he commented that Baja was being released from the terrorist rule of Mexico and that its people were overjoyed. Watkins said the untapped mineral and agricultural resources soon would be properly developed with the help of her sister republic above the border, and that once the conquest had been consolidated, Walker's new nation would be recognized by the United Stated Government. His supporters in San Francisco rejoiced. A new ship, the *Anita,* was purchased with more funds solicited from his supporters, and two hundred fifty new recruits were enlisted.

Meanwhile, Lieutenant Pineada had received no reply to his appeal for help from the Mexican Army detachment. Resorting to subterfuge, he enlisted the help of a prostitute who was angry at being paid by one of the soldiers in Sonoran currency. To her next client from Walker's band, she confidentially reported that the Mexican Army detachment to the north was very large and that more than one thousand troops were marching on La Paz.

President Walker sent word to Vice-President Watkins in San Francisco to speed up the recruiting, and told him that because of military expediency, he was moving the temporary capital of Sonora to Santa Cruz. He then looted the city of all the Yankee dollars and

Mexican pesos that he could find, boarded his band back onto the *Caroline,* and sailed off, still carrying the governor of La Paz in the brig. Off the tip of Baja he spotted what appeared to be a warship, so he passed Santa Cruz and put in at Magdalena Bay. The Indians there were friendly when Walker first arrived, becoming unfriendly when the army attempted to buy fruit with Sonoran paper money. Walker was hopelessly outnumbered there. He moved on.

His next port of call was Ensenada, less than one hundred kilometers from the U.S. border. This was a matter of military strategy, he explained in his next message to the Vice-President: He would consolidate the territory closer to his line of supply. The good citizens of Ensenada also were delighted to see a fresh ship in port. They clapped and cheered as Walker led his men in parade through the community and as he evicted one Paco Gastelum from the town's finest dwelling, appropriated for use as his own headquarters and renamed Fort McKibbon. There seemed to be no objection to this by the Ensenadaens, because the Gastelums were considered to be too rich anyway. Oddly, in Ensenada the merchants accepted the Sonoran currency, possibly because they were told that it was as good as a dollar in the United States.

Trouble for General (President) Walker arose on a different front. Walker dispatched several of his band to "commandeer" horses, cattle, and food from the countryside, and almost immediately they came across La Grulla Ranch. Melendrez and most of his band were on a foraging mission up near Mexicali, and those members of his gang that were left behind were outnumbered by the Walker band. They put up no fight when the Walker men relieved them of their horses, cattle, and most of the food at the ranch. Melendrez and about fifty of his men arrived at La Grulla minutes after the Walker band had departed. Melendrez and his bandits set off in pursuit. They caught up with the Walker band a short distance from the ranch, ambushed it, and killed three or four of the men before the remainder fled back to Ensenada, abandoning their horses, cattle, and food.

Walker retaliated; he immediately had his men round up the citizens of Ensenada and bring them to Fort McKibbon, where he "talked to the people." He had come only to protect them from the outrages of their own government, he said. His sole objective was the amelioration of their own social and political conditions. By all the arts which conduce to civilization, he continued, he desired to render them free from the curse of the Mexican Republic, which was not strong enough to protect them, yet was strong enough to eat up the products of their industry. No bandit would be permitted to disgrace the flag of the new Sonoran Republic, whereas plundering bands of wandering robbers even then were attempting to destroy the saviors.

It was a beautiful speech. A copy of it was sent to Vice-President Watkins for release in San Francisco. Few persons understood what Walker was saying, and while he was delivering his speech the Mexican governor from La Paz bribed the skipper of the *Caroline* to take him back home. No sooner had news of this calamity been reported to Walker then he was informed that two more of his men had been picked off by sniper fire from bandits on the outskirts of Ensenada. Local residents told Walker that Melendrez had a virtual army of bandits and that if he attacked the city all would be lost. Other residents then passed on the information that Colonel Negrete, who had been in Tia Juana during the landing, was returning from that city at the head of a band of soldiers. Colonel Negrete was indeed returning to Ensenada from Tia Juana. His detachment, however, consisted of one cannon and twenty soldiers, and he was not at first inclined to engage in a fight with the Walker band. While he was camped midway between Tia Juana and Ensenada, he received word of the confrontation between Melendrez and Walker. Negrete welcomed the news. He sent a courier to Melendrez with a suggestion that they team up to rid Mexico of this Yankee bandit, and Melendrez, still irritated over Walker's attack on La Grulla Ranch, thought the idea an excellent one. Negrete moved on to Ensenada from the north. Melendrez surrounded the city to the east and to the south. The *Caroline* sailed happily toward La Paz.

The encounter was not of long duration. In it Walker's band suffered thirteen casualties, eight dead and five wounded. Negrete lost three men from his army detachment, and one of the bandits was wounded. Melendrez and Colonel Negrete conferred in person. They agreed that a fight was not necessary. Walker's men were deployed around the northern edge of the town at the base of two small hills. Between those two hills ran a small stream, from which the freebooters were getting their water. A few miles to the east, the stream divided into a Y. It was a comparatively simple manner to post a few snipers on the tops of the hills to keep Walker's men from passing through the canyon back into the city, then dam the tributary of the stream that flowed through his camp.

The siege lasted for eight days, until a desperate Walker's luck began to change. First, a rare fall thunderstorm swept across the desert. The pressure from the runoff waters collapsed the dam. Under cover of the storm, Walker's gang killed three of the hilltop snipers and wounded five others. During the height of the storm, the *Anita* arrived in Ensenada with two hundred fifty heavily armed reinforcements for Walker. The solitary canyon of the Mexican Army became bogged down in the Ensenada adobe mud. Negrete and Melendrez were much too practical to emulate the fabled Spartans. Between them they had fewer arms and fewer men than the filibustering Walker. With a Latin shrug, they abandoned their cannon and drifted away, Negrete to Tia Juana and a well-deserved vacation in San Diego, and Melendrez back into the mountains with his men. A greatly relieved Walker moved back into his warm, comfortable Fort McKibbon.

The administration of the new Republic lasted three months in Ensenada. Walker admirably played the role required of a head of state. He issued decrees, attended reviews, and through Vice-President Watkins sounded out the U.S. State Department on the possibility of a diplomatic interchange. There were some problems, of course. Walker proclaimed that the new Sonoran dollar was worth the same as one Yankee dollar, but three soldiers were buying them at the rate of fifty to one. Accused of undermining the faith of the people in their new currency, they were stripped of their stripes and sent back to the United States in disgrace.

Walker's greatest problem, however, was Melendrez. The Yankee bandit had too many men for Melendrez to attack head on. Periodically, however, one of the bandits would pick off a soldier. Whenever a detachment was sent into the hills to look for Melendrez, no trace of him could be found. Walker took a calculated risk. He sent two hundred of his men to comb the area where the bandit was believed to be hidden. At no time had he learned that La Grulla Ranch was Melendrez's headquarters. While Walker's band was in the hills, Melendrez and his men slipped into Ensenada. They cleaned the army's mess hall of a week's supply of provisions and were gone before the theft was discovered.

Toward the end of the third month, a United States warship, *Portsmouth,* came into Ensenada harbor with an answer to Walker's bid for recognition. President Fillmore had no wish to interfere with Walker's manifest destiny, the skipper told President Walker, but

would President Walker get the hell out of Ensenada and quit embar-
rassing the United States Government. Walker's alternative is not
known, but he did decide to accede to Fillmore's wishes. With the
announcement that Ensenada would forever more be known as the
cradle of Sonoran liberty, and that this part of the campaign was now
well secured, he appointed a grocer as governor general and gave the
keys of Fort McKibbon to him. He divided his army into three groups.
One he sent to San Vincente and another to El Rosario, to solidify the
government in those communities. The fate of these two detach-
ments is not known, but it is assumed that most of the men drifted
back to the United States during the ensuing months. The third
group, made up of the best one hundred men in the army, came
under the personal leadership of the President and General Walker
and set out for the long and dreary march across the desolate dunes
of Camino del Diablo to establish a seat of government for the new
Republic in Sonora. As soon as Walker had departed, the newly
appointed governor general turned back the keys of Fort McKibbon
to its original owner and his authority to the old alcalde and went back
to his grocery business.

Walker's division consisted of one hundred men. On his way out
of Ensenada, he paused again at La Grulla Ranch and confiscated
every horse that he could lay his hands on, and more than one
hundred cattle, still apparently not realizing that this was the headquarters for the bandit who had caused him so much trouble. If he
had, he might have understood why the indignant bandit and his men
trailed his army. By the time the Walker band had crossed the rugged
mountains of the peninsula, it had lost two men, four horses, and
twenty head of cattle. Not one casualty was suffered by the harassing
bandidos. The frustrated Walker decided to adopt the practice used
by Hernan Cortes when he impressed the Toltecs into his army on the
march to Mexico City. Thus, when the Sonoran army emerged on the
lowlands and came on a small Indian village, Walker enlisted thirty
Cocopa Indians in the service of his Republic. The Indians were
delighted to serve in the cause. Walker announced to his men that this
was another indication that all people were tired of the oppression of
their Mexican government. His band with its new personnel renewed
its trek. The following morning, when the army arose, it discovered
that all the Indians had deserted, taking with them thirty head of
cattle plus all the rations for the group. Walker angrily sent some of
his men back to the Indian village. This splinter group returned in

less than two hours, carrying two bodies. It had been ambushed by Melendrez.

Walker continued his trip to the east. They reached the Colorado River, and Walker's men drove the cattle into that wide stream in an attempt to force them to swim across. About half of the cattle drowned and were swept into the Gulf. That night, as the band camped on the eastern bank of the Colorado, a large segment of the group apparently had second thoughts about its role in Walker's manifest destiny. By morning, fifty-two men had reached a decision. Without so much as a nod to their leader, they left the camp and marched north to Fort Yuma in the United States. With more than a thousand miles to go to the seat of the new government, the army of one hundred had dwindled to forty-three and had lost most of its food. Walker wisely decided that it would be more practical to move back into Baja.

He lost some more cattle when he recrossed the Colorado River. His band now was smaller than that of Melendrez: forty-three as compared to the bandit's sixty horsemen. By evening, Walker reached the Rancho Guadalupe of the Osios, which he "captured, with little difficulty." He decided that his men needed rest and that he should camp there for a few days. The men, however, got little rest. Melendrez hid his men in the rugged terrain surrounding the ranch and kept up a sporadic sniper fire during the night. Shortly after dawn, Walker decided to counterattack, and ordered twenty-five men to wipe them out. The snipers prudently withdrew, and the twenty-five-man army set off in pursuit.

Melendrez and his bandits then raced into the village from the opposite direction, guns blazing. The eighteen American bandits still in Rancho Guadalupe hid in a small adobe building and watched Melendrez round up the remaining cattle and drive them off toward the mountains. So outnumbered were they that not one dared fire a shot and so betray his hiding place to the bandit. It was an intelligent decision. The twenty-five-man detail sent after the snipers gave up its chase about five miles from the village and turned back. About two miles from the tiny town, they rode into an ambush. Ten more were slain. When the survivors realized that they were completely encircled, they threw down their arms and raised their hands and surrendered. Melendrez wanted no prisoners, however, He was an honest bandit, not a soldier. He merely took their horses and pistols, and motioned for the survivors to hike back to the village on foot.

For three days, Walker and the thirty-two survivors of his band remained in the Rancho Guadalupe, seeing no sign of the dreaded bandit Melendrez. Then, knowing that they could not remain on the ranch indefinitely, the band marched out into the desert. They moved about ten miles toward San Vincente before they spotted the *bandidos* to the west. This time the Mexicans' behavior seemed different, as if they purposely wanted to be seen: Four of them sat on horseback, motionless, with hands rested on the saddlehorns. Panic-stricken, the men started to run back in the direction of the ranch, then again halted abruptly. Four other bandits, in the east, sat on their horses in the almost identical pose. There were none to the north. Slowly and fearfully, the bedraggled survivors began to move in this direction. Within a matter of a few hours, it became clear to Walker what Melendrez was doing. Every time Walker attempted to turn his men in the direction of Ensenada or San Vincente, the four horsemen would materialize in the distance. Only when he turned them toward the north would they disappear. They were being herded toward the United States border, almost in the same manner in which cattle are driven into a corral.

Some days later, Walker and his army struggled into the bustling border town of Tia Juana. The men had no money; they were hungry and tired. On the outskirts of the city, Walker pulled them all together and gave each one an IOU for back wages and rations allowance, drawn on the treasury of the nonexistent Republic. He then told them all to cross the border and go back to San Francisco, where they would receive further orders. As for himself, Walker said, he would slip through the lines of the enemy and get back to San Vicente.

Walker's men split up, avoided the legal point of entry, and slipped back into the United States by wading across the shallow Tia Juana River. Walker still had some Yankee dollars in his possession. Whether he really planned to attempt to reach San Vincente is unknown. His immediate plans, however, are known. As soon as the last of his men had disappeared, Walker removed the insignia of general of the Sonoran Republic from his dusty khaki uniform, walked boldly into the center of town, and checked into the community's best hotel. His first act there was to order the porter to fetch the city's best tailor. His second act was to bathe in the hostelry's only tub.

When he returned to his hotel room, Colonel Negrete was sitting on the bed. Also in the room were three Mexican soldiers. The

Mexican colonel was in a hurry, so much so that he could not allow Walker time to get dressed. Wearing only a thin summer "union suit," Walker was paraded under guard out of the hotel and into the street. It seemed as if the whole town had turned out to watch the spectacle. The Mexican men laughed uproariously and the *señoritas* giggled uncontrollably as the scantily clad Walker was marched to the port of entry at the United States border, where he was arrested by U.S. authorities.

Walker and Watkins were tried in San Francisco and were found guilty of violating the United States neutrality laws. Each was fined fifteen hundred dollars but this was allowed to go by default. Oddly, both men were treated as heroes in the city by the Golden Gate. The same treatment was accorded the men he had left in Tia Juana when they arrived in San Francisco to collect on their IOUs. Under these circumstances, they apparently forgot their humiliating experience with the band of Mexican bandits, for when Walker proposed another expedition—to liberate the oppressed people of Nicaragua—almost all the survivors signed on.

Walker's adventures in Nicaragua were much better known than his four-month fiasco in Baja, California. He did set himself up successfully as president of that Central America nation. He was thrown out of the country and tried it all over again. The Nicaraguans then became tired of the same old game, and ended it by standing Walker up against the wall and filling him with bullets.

Negrete wrote another letter to the authorities in Mexico City, suggesting that Melendrez be commissioned a general in the army and that his men be enlisted. Melendrez took his commission seriously. He patrolled the whole northern Baja peninsula for several years, allowing no bandit to operate successfully in his area. He died an old and wealthy man at his La Grulla ranch.

A second later, the concussion from the tremendous blast threw Roy on top of his brother, Ray, and toppled them both to the ground.

The De Autremont Brothers

THE first train robbery in the United States took place in 1866 near Seymour, Indiana. The bandits were three brothers named Reno who held up an Ohio and Mississippi express in the mistaken belief that it carried forty thousand dollars in gold. The mail clerk was killed in the futile robbery, thrown from the mail car while the train was moving. The last train robbery in the United States occurred in 1923 near Siskiyou, Oregon. The bandits were three brothers named DeAutremont, and they, like the Renos, believed they would find a gold shipment worth at least forty thousand dollars.

The Renos have been kissed off by historians as three inept hoodlums, but a picture is being painted in some area of the West which portrays the DeAutremonts as a trio of dashing, fearless bandits, swooping across the Pacific Northwest, striking terror into the hearts of trainmen from Seattle to San Francisco. This reputation is not deserved. Their attack on the "Gold Special" of the Southern Pacific is worth recounting, however, because it shows dramatically the advance in the field of forensic science since the attempted Reno robbery a half century earlier.

Two of the DeAutremont brothers were twins, Ray and Roy, born in 1900 in Williamsburg, Iowa, the sons of a barber. Hugh DeAutremont was born four years later in Lakewood, New Mexico. Ray drifted into the Pacific Northwest, where he briefly became an organizer for the IWW (the Wobblies) in Vancouver, Washington. His brother Roy followed, and soon thereafter came the younger brother Hugh and the itinerant barber, the father, Paul. Another son, Lee, remained in Lakewood with his mother.

Ray served a brief jail term because of his Wobbly activities, but for most of the time the four members of the family lived in the city of Eugene, Oregon, a few miles south of Portland.

The twins worshipped many Western outlaws, particularly Jesse James. When the three brothers managed to scrape up enough money to buy a Nash touring sedan, both Roy and Ray usually referred to the vehicle as their "favorite horse." For several years, the twins drifted around the Pacific Northwest, using Eugene as their base; their father was employed there. Their occupation primarily was that of an itinerant farmhand, picking fruit or helping with a wheat harvest. The mental picture they painted of themselves, however, was that of ruthless desperados, lying under cover, waiting to strike. They were convinced that the only reason they worked as farmhands or in restaurants was to establish a cover under which they could hide after they had committed their audacious holdups. The twins talked incessantly of their "big score," and when Hugh was along, he too was included in their dreams.

The first overt action they took in making their dream a reality occurred on June 2, 1922. The twins had just finished a temporary job on a farm in Yakima, Washington, and, feeling flush, had driven over the mountains to Seattle. While walking along the city's notorious Skid Row, they passed a pawnshop. In the window was a .45-caliber Colt pistol. The two brothers looked at the weapon for a long time before they entered the pawnshop. Guns were cheap in those times; that one cost six dollars. Identification of the purchaser was not required. Roy signed for the pistol under the name of William Elliott, with a fictitious address in Seattle. He also purchased ten dollars' worth of ammunition for the gun.

The following month found all three brothers in Cannon Beach, Oregon, without any money and hungry. Another .45 Colt had been added to their arsenal. It had been purchased in Vancouver, Washington, also under a fictitious name. The ammunition, except for two clips, was gone, used up in target practice in isolated areas along the Columbia River.

The DeAutremont brothers decided to make their first strike. Their victim was to be the elderly proprietor of a small candy shop in Cannon Beach. They cased the job for two or three days. Then Ray got a job washing dishes in a seaside restaurant, and the group decided the candy-store holdup would not be worth the risk of interfering with their big caper.

During the ensuing year, the three brothers continued their pattern of working at odd jobs to get gasoline money. Still another pistol was purchased, and an automatic shotgun. In the summer of 1923, the twins drove out to an isolated area near Portland for some more target practice. They stumbled across some sort of construction project, and inside a small portable cabin they found a quantity of dynamite and a Du Pont plunger-type detonator. They loaded the dynamite and the detonator into their Nash and drove back to Eugene.

It was about this same time that Ray read in a "Wild West" magazine an account of a train holdup by Big Jack Davis, a notorious badman who had operated around northern California and Nevada. The story apparently related the holdup by Davis of the Central Pacific's number-one express near Verdi, Nevada, about twelve miles west of Reno, on November 3, 1870. The train also had been carrying about forty thousand dollars in minted gold.

Davis, with a band of seven cutthroats, hid all day in the brush above Verdi. Shortly after dusk, the gang gathered in the Verdi depot. The train slowed as it passed through the station area, and Davis, along with six other bandits, swung on board. Davis and one other man climbed over the tender into the cab of the locomotive. They forced the fireman and engineer to leap from the train. A half mile down the track, Big Jack brought the express to a halt.

The mail clerk refused to open the door to the mail car, where the gold was stored, but Big Jack had anticipated his reluctance and blew the door from the mail car with a charge of dynamite. The band was back in Virginia City before dawn. Its members were rounded up a few days later after a sheriff was tipped by one of the bandits' girlfriends. Davis was given a ten-year jail sentence for his role in the holdup. (Davis was killed by a guard a few years later during a stage-robbery attempt.)

Ray discussed the story of Big Jack Davis's train robbery with his brother, and it triggered a memory in Roy. He recalled hearing about a Southern Pacific train called the "Gold Special" that left Portland every day for San Francisco. It was reputed to carry up to a quarter million dollars in gold on some occasions. Never did it carry less than forty thousand dollars' worth of gold.

The three brothers thought of the train as a golden opportunity to become rich. This would be their first big caper. The DeAutremonts decided they had a tremendous advantage over their Kansas counterparts. They not only were smarter, they also had mountains in which they could hide safely, or they could use their trusty touring car for a quick getaway if this was more practical. The three brothers were all working when the matter of the "Gold Special" first came up, but each quit his job on the following day to concentrate on the plans for the robbery of the "Gold Special." For the first time in their lives, they felt rich. Roy sent a fifty-dollar money order to his younger brother Lee in New Mexico to "help the boy over a hard knock." A one-room shack in an isolated area near Silverton, Oregon, was rented for use as a headquarters post for the caper. The isolation was required so that the three brothers could practice hip shooting and snap shooting without the noise attracting unwanted attention. Also, it was not too far distant from Albany, so Roy could get in to see his girlfriend.

"I've got a big business deal coming up that's going to make me rich," he told her. He purchased a thirty-thousand-dollar life-insurance policy and named her the beneficiary.

In August, Roy and Ray hopped a freight for Ashland, a pretty town located in an agricultural area in southern Oregon. Its residents were primarily railroad people, however, as Ashland was a division point for the Southern Pacific Railroad. It was there that crews changed for the continued southbound run of trains originating in the north. The twins drifted around Ashland for a couple of days before deciding to go farther south to find the proper site for a holdup. They hopped another southbound freight. About three quarters of an hour later, the freight stopped on the summit of the Siskiyou Mountain Range. The twins slipped from the train, then realized that the engineer had stopped only to test the air brakes of the train before it started down the long grade toward California. Elated, the twins watched the train move on until it disappeared in a distant tunnel. This would be the site for their sensational strike.

They spent the next two nights sleeping in the hills above the tracks. Every southbound train, including the "Gold Special," stopped or almost stopped at the Siskiyou summit. On both days, the "Gold Special" reached the summit at approximately twelve forty-five P.M., making it a forty-five-minute run from Ashland. The train carried no freight cars. Behind the huge locomotive was a ten-thousand-gallon cylindrical tender, followed by a mail and baggage car and then still another baggage car. The number of passenger cars varied from day to day. The enormous locomotive was the pride of the Southern Pacific fleet, a 2-10-2, which among other things meant that the engine had fourteen wheels.

After the train passed on the third day, the twins were convinced that this was the ideal place to carry out their ambush. They returned to Eugene, loaded the faithful Nash with supplies, dynamite, and the detonator caps, wire, and plunger, picked up Hugh, and drove south. Near Siskiyou, they pulled off the road and parked their touring car out of sight in a grove of trees.

It took the three brothers three trips to backpack the dynamite and the detonator up the steep hill to the tunnel site, where they stored it along with some lead-in wire under a pile of brush. They spent another day reconnoitering. During this period, they came across an abandoned one-room building about two miles from the tunnel, and this they decided to use for their command post before the raid. A small cave, its entrance partially blocked by a fallen tree, was chosen for their hideout after the robbery.

The DeAutremonts returned to their car, unloaded the staple food supplies and medical kits they had brought from Eugene, and cached them in their hideout. The following day, the twins hiked into Siskiyou, where they purchased more supplies, passing themselves off as hunters from Portland. Then, for the next two or three days, the brothers just hung around the one-room shack, practicing hip and snap firing with their pistols.

Roy began to worry about the Nash. It was sitting alone in a grove of trees, apparently abandoned. Kids might stumble across it and strip it. It was too good a car to leave unprotected like that. Roy relayed his concern to his brothers, and they agreed. The car no longer should be left in the grove. Hugh would drive it back to Eugene, and the robbery of the "Gold Special" would be postponed until Hugh's return.

All did not go smoothly for Hugh DeAutremont on his return trip. A few miles from Ashland, he ran into a wandering cow, and the beloved Nash had to be towed into the town for repairs that took several days. His allocated ten days passed before he reached Eugene. Where Hugh got his money is unknown, but he remained in Eugene for about a week "whooping it up," according to one newspaper story some time later. Hugh then bought a train ticket back to Ashland. There was no way he could buy a ticket for the remainder of his trip to the Siskiyou summit, and it was while he was waiting to jump on a freight that he was picked up by a Southern Pacific Railroad patrol-man. Hugh insisted he was waiting for a train to go to San Francisco, but the railroad cop was skeptical. He took Hugh into a Southern Pacific office and searched him. Hugh's driving license and a receipt for a premium on the life-insurance policy Roy had taken out in favor of his girlfriend in Albany were noted. Apparently, Hugh had paid the premium during his visit in Eugene.

The railroad cop gave Hugh one of two choices: He could either purchase a ticket to San Francisco or be arrested as a vagrant. Hugh bought the ticket. A couple of hours later, nineteen-year-old Hugh DeAutremont, still sputtering over the treatment he had received from the railroad cop, hopped a freight outside of Ashland for Tunnel 13 on the S.P. tracks at Siskiyou Summit. He rejoined his brothers on October 7, and found them angrily packing up, planning to leave, but they accepted his excuses for his delay and put the robbery plans back into motion.

Another trip was made into Siskiyou, this time to purchase a gallon of creosote, a pound of black pepper, and some greasepaint. Covers for their shoes were made from old gunnysacks and soaked in the creosote. On the 9th and the 10th, the three brothers hiked to the tunnel to watch for the passage of the "Gold Special." On both days it arrived about twelve thirty P.M., slowed to a near stop for the brake testing, then picked up speed as it entered the tunnel. The attack was set for October 11.

The morning of the 11th was spent removing evidence which might link them to the one-room cabin they used as a command post. Two hours before the "Gold Special" was due to arrive, the three brothers arrived at Tunnel 13. They smeared themselves with greasepaint "so that they would think we were Mexicans," tied the creosoted gunnysacks around their feet, and slipped into overalls. They went over the plans of attack again. Each of the brothers repeated aloud his part in the action. The maneuver was foolproof.

At noon they split up. Ray, carrying the detonator, went through the tunnel to the south portal, where the dynamite had been stacked. Hugh and Roy hid in the brush a short distance above the tunnel's north portal, where the train hesitated for the routine testing of the air brakes. At twelve twenty P.M., they heard the train puffing up the grade.

The engineer on the Southern Pacific's "Gold Special" on October 11, 1923, was fifty-one-year-old Sidney Bates, of Dunsmuir, California, a veteran of more than twenty years with the S.P. The fireman was Benjamin Seng, forty-six, also from Dunsmuir. Both men had brought a northbound passenger train up from California on the preceding day and spent the night in Ashland, where the crews were changed. The conductor was Andrew Merrett. There is no record of his home town or age. The head brakeman was Raymond Grin, of Ashland. Elvyn Earl Dougherty, the thirty-four-year-old mail clerk on the train, was not on his regular run. He was relieving a fellow mail clerk who had not returned from a hunting trip. Deadheading on the train was another S.P. brakeman, Charles Orrin Johnson. Johnson and Dougherty were also from Ashland. Existing records disclose the names of only two of the passengers, Herbert Micander and Edward O. Joers, although there must have been many, because the train was pulling eight or nine passenger cars in addition to baggage and mail cars. Joers was a medical student.

Bates, as was his practice, slowed the train to a near halt as it reached Siskiyou Summit and he tested the brakes. He switched on the locomotive bell. Regulations required that the bell be rung whenever an S.P. train approached and passed through a tunnel. Then he saw a curious sight. Two men, clad in bibbed overalls, their faces smeared with greasepaint and their shoes swathed in gunnysacks, awkwardly ran from the brush toward the train. The engineer wanted no bums like these riding the "Gold Special." He pushed the throttle forward, and the wheels of the locomotive spun on the smooth tracks as steam filled the cylinders. The train slowly gathered speed.

For almost a minute, Roy thought that they were not going to make it. It was most difficult to run with the gunnysacks tied around his feet. Hugh leaped for the handbar on the front of the first freight car, caught it, and held on. Roy lost his gun. It fell from the waistband of his pants and slid down through the pants of his overalls. He could not stop to recover it. He dove for the handbars at the rear of the first freight car, caught the bottom one, and received a painful wrench in the shoulder as he scrambled onto the train.

The train was approximately two miles from the north portal when Ray and Hugh boarded it. It was less than three hundred yards from the entrance when the two brothers slithered over the locomotive tender into the locomotive cab. Hugh held his pistol pointed toward the two crewman, but it was Roy who gave the orders. "Pull the train to a stop so that the mail car is just inside the tunnel's south portal," he ordered.

Bates quickly agreed to do as the two apparitions ordered. The train came to a stop as the locomotive emerged from the south end of the tunnel. The dynamite was stacked in a pile beside Ray, who waited inside the tunnel near the entrance.

Dougherty slid open the door of the mail car and looked out curiously. At the same time, Ray fired one hip shot from his shotgun at the mail clerk. Dougherty slammed the door shut. The charge missed him by several feet.

After ordering Hugh to keep the engineer and fireman "in his gunsight," Roy clambered down from the locomotive. The gunnysacks around his feet were cumbersome, and he took them off, then ran to the mail car. The execution of the plan was moving perfectly, he thought, although the noise from the clanging locomotive bell was piercing in the tunnel. He yelled to Hugh to have the engineer turn it off, but no one could hear him. Ray tossed him a stick of dynamite, and he wedged it in the door of the mail car. Ray tossed him another stick, and another, and another. The dynamite kept coming, and Roy tamped it all around the door. When the door was completely plugged, he put the remainder of the stolen dynamite on top of the previously planted sticks. Roy then attached wire to the detonator caps, jumped down, and ran back to the Du Pont activator. The plan called for Ray to trigger the blast, but Roy could not wait. He jammed down the plunger.

A second later, the concussion from the tremendous blast threw him on top of Ray and toppled them both to the ground. For a few seconds the twins lay stunned on the cinders, their ears ringing, and greasepainted faces bleeding from the flying pebbles. Groggily, they struggled to their feet, then stared at the mail car in amazement. It had been blown apart. Dougherty's body was shredded and splattered onto the wall of the tunnel. The interior of the mail car burned furiously, and the tunnel was filled with dense smoke, dynamite fumes, and steam that left the twins choking and gasping for breath.

Ray staggered out of the tunnel. Roy ran after him.

Andrew Merrett, the conductor on the "Gold Special," was sitting in the smoker, the sixth car behind the engine, when the mail car exploded. The window beside him was shattered, and the flying glass slashed open his cheek. There was sudden silence in the smoker, a silence that was accented by the frightened cries of a young woman in the car behind the smoker. Holding a handkerchief to his cheek to stem the bleeding, he stepped down from the smoker and went to the rear of the train, which still was well outside the tunnel. Black smoke and steam poured out from the tunnel entrance.

At the rear of the train, he joined the two brakemen, Grin and Johnson, and passenger Herbert Micander. After a few minutes' conversation, they concluded that the boiler on the locomotive had exploded. Lighting some red emergency flares, the four men entered the tunnel to investigate. A few minutes later, they came across the wreckage of the burning mail car and the mangled body of the young mail clerk. The smoke and fumes were suffocating, and the four men stumbled back to the north portal. As soon as they had gulped in fresh air, Johnson paused. "You go see if there is a doctor on the train," he said to Micander. "As soon as I get my breath back, I'm going to report to the engineer."

Roy and Ray DeAutremont waited outside the south portal of the tunnel for the smoke to clear. Beside them, up in the cab, was Hugh, with his pistol still pointed toward Bates and Seng. Roy waited impatiently for about ten minutes. Finally, he borrowed Ray's pistol and ran back into the tunnel. Their plan of operation called for uncoupling the mail car from the first freight car: then they would have the engineer pull it down the tracks for a couple of miles, where it could be rifled at leisure. Although the interior of the mail car now was a mass of flames, Roy had been programmed sufficiently to continue with the operation. He could not, however, uncouple the car. He groped and fumbled with the stubborn coupling for several minutes, but could not separate the two cars. He paused, then swore softly as he heard footsteps approaching from the rear of the train. A moment later, he spotted a small red light bobbing in the murk. Presently he made out the duckbilled hat of the brakeman, Charles Johnson.

Roy pointed his gun. "Come over here and show me how to uncouple this train," he snarled. He was becoming angry. The uncoupling was a necessary part of the plan, and it followed the pattern described in the "Wild West" magazine which had reported the successful Kansas robbery.

Johnson walked closer to Roy, his hands over his head. He carefully detailed the mechanics of the coupling, explaining that the cars could not be separated unless the train was slowly moving ahead.

Roy accepted this explanation. "Keep your hands over your head," he said. "Go down to the locomotive cab and tell my brother to have the engineer pull ahead."

Johnson did as he was told. When he stepped out of the tunnel, however, Ray gave him no time to speak. He shot him in the stomach with his automatic shotgun. Johnson fell to the ground, screaming. Hugh, hearing the cries, pushed his head out of the cab, saw what had happened, and silenced Johnson by shooting him twice with his pistol.

Roy heard the gunfire and guessed what had happened. He left the mail car, stumbled to the south portal, and reported what the brakeman had said about the coupling process. The DeAutremonts were becoming nervous. The engine bell still pealed eerily in the crisp mountain air. At least ten minutes had elapsed since the train had been stopped. Some of the passengers in the rear of the train could already be running to Siskiyou to spread word of the holdup.

He called out to Hugh and told him to have the engineer pull the train forward. Bates advanced the throttle, but the train would not budge. Bates knew what had happened. The train was equipped with air brakes. Air pressure kept the brake shoes away from the wheels of the train. When the pressure was lowered, the brakes were applied. When the air pressure was raised, the shoes were pushed away from the wheels. The dynamite blast had ruptured the air-pressure-storage system of the train. With no pressure, the brakes were clamped against the wheels. Bates attempted to explain the system to Hugh in the cab.

Angrily, Roy climbed up into the cab to see why Bates would not do as he was told. Once again, Bates explained the braking system and what had happened. Swearing loudly, Roy looked over toward the fireman, Benjamin Seng, who stood near the tender with his hands partially raised. Whipping up his pistol, Roy hip fired two shots at Seng. Both struck the fireman in the head, killing him instantly. His body fell from the cab to the ground below.

Roy leaped from the cab and joined Ray. They both then groped their way back into the tunnel. The smoke and fumes were much worse than they had been when Roy had left the tunnel a few minutes earlier. Flames poured from the ruptured car.

For a few minutes the twins watched the fire rage, with a sinking realization that it would be hours before anyone could get into the wreckage to get the gold. A posse surely would be on their trail before this could be achieved. The twins gave up. They ran out of the tunnel to the locomotive. Ray began throwing pepper on the ground, with the thought that it would stop any hounds from following them. Roy peeled off his overalls and threw them down near the dead fireman. Ray then noticed that Roy had discarded his gunnysacks. Ray discarded his. Hugh watched from the cab, then removed his gunnysacks.

"What are we going to do with the engineer?" Hugh asked.

"Bump him off," Roy replied.

Hugh responded like a professional soldier. He fired a .45-caliber bullet into the back of Sidney Bates's head.

A few minutes later, the three inept train robbers scrambled up the side of the hill near the south portal of Tunnel 13. At the crest of the hill, they paused and looked back. About a dozen men and women were near the one passenger car that had not been pulled into the tunnel. The locomotive protruded from the south portal of the tunnel, its bell still ringing loudly enough to be heard at the top of the hill. Smoke poured out of the south portal and rose like a signal into the clear, cloudless sky. The time was one thirty P.M.

Grin, Micander, and Merrett had located a medical student, Edward O. Joers, and they had just entered the tunnel through the north portal when they heard the gunfire that killed Johnson. Micander apparently was familiar with the country in southern Oregon, and he struck off for help in Siskiyou. Grin and Merrett and Joers slowly returned to the end of the train, where many of the passengers had gathered. Many had heard the gunfire, and all knew what was happening at the other end of the train. Oddly, none of the passengers tried to run; neither was there any sign of panic. A woman first noticed the three bandits climbing up the side of the hill, and after they had been pointed out, Joers, Grin, and Merrett again entered the tunnel. They found the four victims of the DeAutremont brothers a few minutes later.

The hideout chosen by the DeAutremonts was a little less than two miles from Tunnel 13, but the three brothers could not find it. Several weeks had passed since their last visit to the cave, and each had a different opinion as to its location. For hours the trio floundered through the woods, snapping and snarling at one another. They found it shortly before dusk, before they had come to blows, and each thought he had been right in determining its location. Exhausted, they crawled over the fallen tree into their sanctuary. There was no sign of pursuit.

Details of the immediate search for the three brothers are incomplete and contradictory. Some reports contend that a posse was formed and was on the trail by early afternoon, but this is unlikely. Other reports contend that only roadblocks were set up in the area, because of the logical assumption that the murderers had escaped by car. Jack Pement of the Oregon *Journal*, who is an expert on this robbery, states that the ground search was thorough and even Army Air Corps planes conducted an aerial hunt for the bandits.

By the following morning, Southern Pacific detectives from both Portland and San Francisco were at the site. The pistol lost by Roy when he jumped onto the train was found, as were the discarded overalls and creosoted gunnysacks. If any notice was made of the pepper, it went unreported. The tangible clues were sent on to San Francisco. The serial numbers on the missing gun were traced to a William Elliott in Seattle, and the name and address were quickly checked and found to be fictitious.

The overalls were turned over to a forensic expert, Dr. Edward Oscar Heinrich, at the University of California in Berkeley. The Du Pont detonator was traced to Portland, where its theft had been reported.

The day after he had received the overalls, Dr. Heinrich called the Southern Pacific detectives to his office for what he termed a preliminary report. "From my analysis of substances found on and in the overalls, such as hairs, dust, pitch," the forensic expert said, "I have reached the following conclusions. The owner is a white man, between twenty-three and twenty-five, about five feet ten inches tall, weight about one hundred sixty-five pounds, medium light brown hair, fair complexion, small feet and hands, and he is left-handed." Heinrich missed Roy's weight by about twenty pounds and was wrong on his being left-handed. Otherwise, the description of Roy DeAutremont was uncannily accurate.

"From my analysis of a piece of flimsy paper found in the bottom of the narrow pencil pocket of the overall's bib," Heinrich continued, "I conclude that one of the suspects you seek is a Roy DeAutremont who a month ago was living in Eugene, Oregon." The forensic expert passed a piece of paper to the nonplussed detectives. It was a receipt for the fifty-dollar postal money order sent by Roy to his younger brother Lee in Lakewood, New Mexico.

Three days after the multiple murders, police arrived at the Eugene home of Paul DeAutremont, father of the three killers. They found him worried over his sons' long absence on a hunting trip. Police searched the house. Hairs taken from one of Roy's sweaters were sent to Heinrich. They matched the hairs on the abandoned overalls. A handwriting expert in Portland matched the handwriting of the William Elliott of Seattle who had purchased the .45-caliber pistol with the signature of Roy DeAutremont. The storekeeper in Siskiyou recalled the twins who had purchased supplies and a quantity of creosote from him. The Southern Pacific officer who had picked up Hugh DeAutremont sent in his notes. One of the passengers on the ambushed "Gold Special" told of three men he had seen at the top of the hill about an hour after the train was stopped.

Less than a week after the holdup and murders, posters offering $14,400 in reward for the arrest of the DeAutremont brothers were being posted all over the United States.

In a copyrighted interview with Jack Pement for a series of articles in the Oregon *Journal* a half century after the ambush, Ray DeAutremont claimed that he and his brothers remained in their "cache" for about twelve days. This series of interviews with the highly competent Pement is the only record of what happened to the DeAutremonts immediately after the killings.

After twelve days in the hideout, the DeAutremonts' food began to run low. They decided that Ray should leave the hideout, go to Eugene, pick up the Nash touring car, and return to rescue his brothers. Ray hiked to the Southern Pacific tracks and waited near Tunnel 13 for a northbound train. In running to catch this train, he lost his Colt .45, in the same way that Roy had lost his. He made no attempt to recover it.

He slipped off the freight car as it approached the city of Medford and went into a restaurant near the railroad depot. He sat at the counter and ordered a cup of coffee. A man entered, sat down beside him, and opened up a copy of the Oregon *Journal.* Ray nearly choked on his coffee when he saw a page-one headline asking, HAVE YOU SEEN THE DEAUTREMONT TWINS?

Leaving his coffee behind, Ray quietly slipped away from the café. He went to the Medford post office. The reward poster, with pictures of himself, Roy, and Hugh, was prominently displayed in the post-office lobby. The thought occurred to him, quite correctly, that he never would see his Nash touring car again. He hiked out of Medford. The following day he got a job picking pears in a nearby community named Central Point. He worked there for about a week, long enough to pick up some wages, then returned to the hideout.

The brothers waited another couple of days in their hideout, believing that their identities had been discovered through the S.P. policeman who had picked up Hugh in Ashland shortly before the raid. According to Ray, the brothers left their hideout eighteen days after the killings. They still carried the automatic shotgun and one .45 pistol as they hiked and hopped freights into California. Ray parted from his brothers in the small town of Hornbrook, leaving with Roy as contact a general-delivery post-office address. Hugh and Roy continued on to Grenada, where they parted.

The three brothers avoided capture for four years. Hugh joined the army and was sent to the Philippines. In 1927, a corporal named Thomas Reynolds saw a faded DeAutremont wanted poster in the San Francisco post office and recognized Hugh as a soldier he had known in Manila as James C. Price. Hugh was arrested in Manila on February 11, 1927. He was returned to Oregon the following month and charged with first-degree murder.

The Southern Pacific Railroad reprinted the reward posters, this time with only the pictures of the twins on them. Eventually, one of the posters was seen in the post office at Portsmouth, Ohio, by an Albert Collingsworth He told the recently formed Federal Bureau of Investigation that the wanted men looked a lot like Elmer and Clarence Goodwin, two men with whom he had worked with at nearby Hanging Rock.

At first, when they were arrested on June 8, 1927, the Goodwins denied that they were the DeAutremonts, but when they realized that they were going to be taken to Oregon, Elmer admitted that he was Ray and that Clarence was indeed Roy. They were arrested in Steubenville, Ohio. Ray, some eighteen months earlier, had married sixteen-year-old Hazel Sprouse and had fathered a child. She knew him only as Elmer Goodwin. All had lived together in the same house. Ray said that for several months they had drifted around California before leaving for what they thought would be the safest part of the Midwest.

When Roy and Ray were brought to Jacksonville, Oregon, a short time later, Hugh's trial was in progress. The twins, both jaunty and in good spirits, pleaded "not guilty" at their arraignment.

The crime was almost four years old when Hugh's trial ended—time enough for tempers to have cooled. Hugh was found guilty, but the jury was merciful and sentenced him to life imprisonment in the Oregon State Penitentiary instead of the expected hanging. When Ray and Roy heard of Hugh's reprieve, they indulged in some plea bargaining with the prosecutor's office and switched their pleas to "guilty" in return for similar life sentences.

In 1949, Roy DeAutremont was diagnosed as hopelessly schizophrenic and was transferred from the State Prison to the Oregon State Hospital for the Insane. Hugh was paroled in November, 1958. He went to San Francisco and got a job as a printer, but died six months later, a victim of cancer. Ray DeAutremont was paroled in October, 1961. Since that time he has worked as a part-time janitor at the University of Oregon, and at this writing lives in a small rented cottage in Eugene. Roy is still confined in the State Hospital

Ironically, the only DeAutremont to die violently was baby brother Lee, to whom Roy had sent fifty dollars shortly before the attempted train robbery. He was shot in a poolroom brawl in Texas in 1926.

There is another ironic twist to the last train holdup in the United States. There was no gold on board the train, nor had there ever been any sizable gold shipment. The train officially was known in Southern Pacific records as "Train 13." Then how did it get its nickname?

When the Portland-San Francisco service first was started, Train 13 was advertised as the "Golden Gate (California) Special." From this it was corrupted to the "Gold Special."

It was an end of an era in the American West, an era launched by Tom Bell some sixty years earlier. Kuhl was the last man to hold up a stagecoach.

Tom Bell and Benjamin Kuhl

THE association of highwaymen and bandits of the West with the careening stagecoach as their quarry has become so rooted in Western legend that it is difficult to realize that only sixty years elapsed between the first stage holdup and the last. The first holdup was engineered by a notorious

Western badman, who used the alias Tom Bell, and it took place in northern California on August 11, 1856. Although it was not successful, it triggered the wrath of so many citizens that it led directly to the capture of the pseudo Bell and his subsequent hanging.

The last holdup occurred in Nevada. It was successful. The bandit was Benjamin Kuhl, who made his mark on Western history on December 5, 1916. Kuhl also was caught, but not before he was able to bury the loot from his robbery somewhere near the Nevada ghost town of Jarbidge.

There was a real Tom Bell. He was a small-time confidence man, a card cheat, thief, and occasional robber. Mild-mannered and fawning in nature, he avoided violence in which he might be involved, but he sought out the company of outlaws and cutthroats. It was in a tavern known as Murderers' Bar in Murphy's Diggings, a hangout for desperados, that Tom Bell, over a game of monte, met a young doctor newly arrived from the Deep South named Thomas J. Hodges. It was a chance meeting, and there is no record of the two men ever meeting again. Yet that casual encounter was to make the name of Tom Bell famous in the roster of notorious Western outlaws.

Not much is known about Hodges's early life, other than that he came from Nashville, Tennessee. Neither is it known whether he really was a doctor. He was accepted as a medical attaché when the Tennessee Volunteers joined in the U.S. invasion of Mexico, and after his return he hung up his shingle briefly in Nashville. No record ever has been found to indicate his attendance at a medical school, but at the time it was possible to get almost any type of diploma by mail. It is known that he made no pretense of practicing medicine after his arrival in California.

He was a tall man, with broad shoulders. His hair was thick and long, and he wore the heavy sideburns and beard that were popular in that era. He was not a handsome man. At some time during his Mexican venture his nose had been broken. Some reports say he was struck by a rifle butt. Others claim the injury was caused by a saber, but all reports said the broken nose gave him a "ferocious mien" that struck fear in all who faced him.

Extremely sensitive about his appearance, he was known to flail out wildly at anyone who mentioned his injury. On one occasion, near Yuba City, he shot and wounded a man who had merely asked how his nose had become broken. As his reputation spread, the Sacramento *Union* described him as a man who showed no mercy to his victims. "He carries six revolvers and several bowie knives and wears a breast plate of thin border iron around his body," the newspaper said.

When he first came to California, he took up placer mining, but this apparently didn't pan out. He then slipped into the role of a highwayman. According to some reports, he used a flour sack with holes cut out for the eyes as a head mask to hide his distinctive appearance. In this early stage of his career, he was a loner, striking at solitary travelers or single freight wagons, and the receipts from his robberies were small. In June of 1855, Hodges held up a freight wagon near Auburn, then cantered away directly into the arms of three deputy sheriffs en route to Auburn. He was arrested and taken to the city jail in Auburn, where the jailer asked him his name.

For some reason, Hodges remembered the young man with whom he had played monte a few weeks earlier in Murderers' Bar. "Tom Bell," he replied. With that answer, Tom Hodges, the former doctor from Nashville, Tennessee, disappeared and a new Tom Bell came into being. He was tried for the robbery as Tom Bell, convicted, and jailed in Angels Island Prison in San Francisco Bay as Tom Bell.

Hodges-Bell did not remain in Angels Island Prison very long. A week after he was admitted, he became seriously ill. He could barely rise from the cot in his cell. The turnkey reported his illness to the warden, who, after a couple of days of observation, decided that his new prisoner was indeed dying. He arranged to have Hodges-Bell transferred to the county jail in San Francisco, where medical treatment was more readily available.

The convict did not respond quickly to medical care in his new jail. For several weeks he shared a special cell set aside for the sick with William Gristy, who was also known as Bill White. Gristy was a convicted cattle rustler and horse thief, and he and Hodges-Bell became as good friends as any could be in their chosen profession.

Whether Hodges-Bell was really sick or, because of his medical background, was successfully feigning an illness is unknown. Most historians assume that he was faking his illness. The nature of Gristy's complaint has never been determined. It is known, however, that both men made miraculous recoveries. On the recommendation of the attending physician, they were allowed to walk in the prison yard for exercise. They walked right out of the prison gate, and when their disappearance was noticed, both convicts were safely hidden in the warrens of the infamous Barbary Coast in San Francisco.

It was there that Hodges-Bell formed the nucleus of his first gang. It included Ned Conners and Jim Smith, who also were escapees from the San Francisco jail and friends of Gristy's. Hodges-Bell recruited three other members: Montague Lyon, better known as Monte Jack, Juan Fernandez, and Bob Cart, also known as English Bob. Singly and in pairs, the seven men drifted out of San Francisco and rendezvoused at a prearranged location in the foothills north of Auburn.

In the beginning, they did not operate as a band. Working in pairs, they held up solitary travelers and unguarded freight trains, much in the same manner as Hodges-Bell had done before he was caught. Now, however, the robbers always identified themselves as part of "Tom Bell's band," sometimes crying it out over and over to make sure the victim got the message.

The real Tom Bell, harassed and frustrated, sadly left for southern California, where he eventually was killed in an argument arising from a card game. Some sources contend that the real Tom Bell tried to cash in on the notoriety arising over his name and started some banditry on his own. If he did, he did not continue with it. Records show that Tom Bell was killed in the game room of the Bella Union Hotel in Los Angeles in January of 1856.

The pseudo Bell, meanwhile, kept his activities limited to a general area between the communities of Folsom and Auburn. He formed an alliance with Jack Phillips, proprietor of a wayside inn known as Mountainair House. Phillips would send word to Bell whenever a well-heeled traveler departed the hostelry. He bought the loot at severely discounted prices from Bell after the robbery.

On several occasions, deputy sheriffs set out to track Bell, but he was always successful in eluding them. They knew for whom they were searching, although the descriptions of the bandits sometimes varied. Most of the victims reported, however, that the leader of the bandit trio or duo was a tall man, more than six feet, with a broken nose and a long sandy mustache that encircled his mouth to join a goatee of the same sandy hue. His long blond hair hung down over his shoulders.

He showed no discrimination in picking his victims. He struck everyone, from a vegetable peddler to a wealthy merchant. One of his victims was a man known as Dutch John, who was carrying a wagon-load of beer from Volcano to Drytown. As the number of his victims swelled, the newspapers of northern California became more and more sarcastic about the inability of lawmen to run this outlaw down.

The Sacramento *Union* editorialized: "What is the result of this failure to catch one who is after all only an ordinary man? He is now, doubtless, emulous of the reputation of Joaquin, is striving for the character of the dashing highwayman, and hopes that his life may be written, as Jack Shepard's was after he shall have expiated his crimes upon the gallows."

The newspaper called on the governor to organize a ranger company and go after Bell. Governor Johnson, showing his irritation, replied that the state had no arms at its disposal and that it lacked the power to form a ranger posse to seek out the outlaw. A months-long feud developed between the governor and the newspaper over the proper manner in which to take care of Tom Bell.

Meanwhile, Tom Bell was paying little if any attention to the furor he was raising. More outlaws joined the gang, and Bell expanded the scope of his operations. He entered into an agreement with attractive, red-haired, buxom Elizabeth Hood, the operator of the Western Exchange Hotel on the Sacramento-Nevada City road. The agreement paralleled that which Bell maintained with Jack Phillips of the Mountainair House, except that in very short order Elizabeth became Bell's mistress, and she did not buy the loot obtained from victims she had fingered.

According to Western historian Joseph Henry Jackson, members of the Bell gang made themselves known to Elizabeth Hood by showing her a bullet bored through and hung on a knotted string. When any member of the gang came into her hotel and showed her this talisman, she pointed out to him which of the travelers carried the largest amount of cash. These patrons subsequently were waylaid shortly after they continued their journey. Peace officers noticed a correlation between Mountainair House and the Western Exchange Hotel, and placed a stakeout at both locations in the hope of snaring Bell.

At about this same time, however, Bell and his gang abruptly ceased their operations. At first the lawmen thought this was the aftermath of an incident that occurred at a toll bridge on the Yuba River operated by a man named Woods. Three horsemen rode up to the bridge and told Woods that because times were hard and they were members of Tom Bell's gang, they would not pay the toll. Woods picked up his rifle and fired at the trio, the bullet hitting one of the men. The three men galloped away. Woods rounded up some of his neighbors and started off in pursuit. The posse members caught up with the trio at French Corral, engaged in a brief gun battle, in which no one was apparently hit, then continued after the fleeing bandits. They lost them after nightfall, but picked up the trail the following morning. Early in the forenoon, they came across one of the hideouts for the Bell gang, hastily abandoned. The posse lost much of its ardor when it realized the size of the band it now would have to pursue, and its members returned to their homes.

When several weeks passed without Bell or his men committing any robbery, lawmen wondered if the posse headed by Woods possibly had scattered the outlaw band. It was an erroneous theory, but it was correct in one sense: Bell had trimmed his gang to its original seven—in order to carry out a spectacular robbery.

There had never been a robbery of a stagecoach in the West. In view of the popularity of stagecoach robbery in later years, it is incredible to think that no highwayman had struck at one before this, but the stagecoaches had been left alone. Tom Hodges-Bell was to change all this.

On the morning of August 11, 1856, the regularly scheduled stage pulled out of Camptonville for the long run to distant Marysville. The stage was operated by the Langton Express Company, and, in addition to a full load of passengers, the vehicle carried more than one hundred thousand dollars' worth of gold.

The stagecoach driver was John Gear, and riding shotgun next to him was a man named Dobson. The gold carried on the stage belonged to Jeremiah Rideout, a gold-dust dealer in Camptonville. Rideout had made several such large gold shipments in the past, and it was his habit to accompany the gold all the way to the bank in San Francisco. Thus, when word was leaked to Bell that Rideout was planning a trip to San Francisco on August 11, the outlaw knew that a fortune in gold would be on the stage.

Bell planned his ambush at a spot named Dried Creek, where the roads divided into two separate trails for about three miles. One of the roads followed the high side of the ravine made by the stream. The other followed the lower side, and was considerably shorter than the upper road. The stage always took the lower road. Bell planned to have his band divided into two groups, one on each side of the road. Both would attack the stage simultaneously while Bell took care of the front.

It was not a particularly novel plan of attack, but it probably would have worked had Rideout not been fed up with the close quarters of a swaying, bouncing stagecoach. He had decided to accompany the stage on horseback. It was hot. There had been no rain for several days, and the road was dusty. To escape the dust, Rideout rode ahead of the stage, and by the time he reached Dried Creek, John Gear was more than a mile behind him. When Rideout reached the fork in the road, he paused and looked back. The stage was lost in a cloud of dust. The lower road was in the full glare of the sun. The upper road was shaded by a heavy growth of trees, and because of this, Rideout decided to travel along the upper spur.

His arrival had not gone unnoticed. Bell dispatched three of his men to intercept the gold merchant, rob him, and take his horse so that he could not sound an early warning to lawmen of the stage robbery. He had proceeded about a half mile along the upper road when the three bandits burst from behind a clump of trees. Rideout was forced at gunpoint to dismount. He was searched, but he carried only a very small amount of money.

Rideout's horse was an exceptionally fine animal, but the gold merchant thought it incredible that the three highwaymen should suddenly fall into a dispute over which man was going to keep it. While the argument continued, Rideout slipped unnoticed down the bank and raced over the dry stream bed to intercept the stage.

The ambush started before Rideout reached the lower road. Three more bandits, apparently unaware that their partners had not returned, or not caring, charged out at the stage as it passed the large boulders where they hid. Dobson killed Juan Fernandez instantly with a shot from his rifle. One of the robbers wounded Dobson in the return fire, but then a fusillade of shots broke out from the passenger section of the stage from several of the travelers who were armed. Another of the bandits was wounded, and the third broke away. Tom Bell remained out of sight.

At this point, the three highwaymen who had intercepted Rideout on the upper road appeared on the scene. One was shot out of his saddle by a passenger, and presently another of the robbers was wounded. The two men gave up and raced off across the mesa. Rideout's horse cantered up to the battle scene. The stage was now stopped. There were casualties there also. In addition to Dobson, John Campbell, a passenger, had received a gunshot wound in the head. An unidentified rider had been shot in both legs, and a Mrs.

Barbara Tilghman of Marysville was dead from a bullet wound in the head. The body of the second bandit killed was believed to be that of English Bob.

Although no one saw Tom Bell at the scene, the two dead bandits were known to have been members of his gang, and Tom Bell received all of the blame for the audacious attack and the murder. Public outrage soared over the death of Mrs. Tilghman. Women were a rare commodity in those times, and the slaying of one was a most heinous offense. Citizens and lawmen formed posses, the largest one headed by Captain William King of Marysville. In Sacramento, local authorities assigned Detectives Robert Harrison and Daniel Gay to the case with instructions to do nothing else besides capture and destroy the Bell gang. The posses scoured the entire Mother Lode country searching for the elusive bandit, and although they did not find him, the pressure on Bell was great enough to cause him to write a letter to Marysville's Captain King.

> My dear Captain King,
>
> I think you could make more by not being quite so officious, for I have had opportunities to put several hundred dollars in your pocket. There was the matter of the Walker and the Martin mares for which there was a $400 reward offered. I could have told you where you might find them, but your vigilant search after me keeps me from putting you on to a great many good things. But don't think for a moment that your vigilance causes me any uneasiness, or that I seek an armistice. No, far from it, for I have unfurled my banner to the breeze and my motto is "Catch me if you can!"
>
> Captain, I know you are pretty smart, but I think if you would only travel with me a short time I would teach you some tricks that you have never thought of. I am not guilty of every accusation that is alleged against me. For instance, some malicious scoundrel tried to saddle the murder at Frenchman's Baron to me, but he could not do it. I am too proud to commit such an atrocious and cowardly murder as that was.
>
> Truly yours,
> Tom Bell

It is unknown which murder at Frenchman's Baron Tom Bell referred to. Captain King did not take up Tom Bell's invitation. He turned the letter over to a Marysville newspaper, which published it, and continued his search for the outlaw. In Sacramento, Detective Harrison was given a new partner to replace Gay, who was assigned to another case. The new partner, Jack M. Anderson, and Harrison were tipped one night that a drunk in a riverfront bar was boasting loudly of his association with Tom Bell, and they went to the bar to investigate. The drunk was a man named Tom Brown, and, after a brief interrogation in the Sacramento Police headquarters, the two detectives were convinced that the man was indeed a member of the Bell gang.

Whether Brown acted out of revenge for some unknown reason or did not realize the significance of what he was saying because he had soaked up so much booze was never made public by the two detectives. At the end of the interrogation, however, the two lawmen had learned where five of the Bell gang were hiding, and that one might be Bell himself. They were living in a tent, Brown reported, in the hills above Folsom and not far distant from Mountainair House. Jack Phillips, the unsavory proprietor of the inn, kept them supplied with food and drink.

The following day, Brown was "induced" to cooperate in an attempt by Harrison to pick up the gang members. Two other detectives, whose names are unknown, joined Harrison and Anderson in the raid.

Brown led the four lawmen to the tent, and the attack went off as planned. Brown opened the tent flap, calling out to his friends as he did so, then held the flap up so that Harrison and Anderson could enter. The other two lawmen remained outside as a backup. Four members of the gang were seated at a table, playing poker. A fifth member bent over a mirror, adjusting his necktie. When Harrison and Anderson raised their shotguns, the man at the mirror pulled out his pistol and fired. The bullet passed between the two men. He had time for only the one shot before Harrison squeezed the trigger on his shotgun, killing the man instantly. Three of the poker players slowly raised their hands, but the fourth rolled off the box on which he was seated and vanished under the wall of the tent. Anderson fired in the general direction the man had taken. By the time Anderson got out of the tent and was joined by the two backup men, this outlaw had disappeared. It was not until they questioned the survivors back inside the tent that they learned the identity of the man who had escaped. It was Bill Gristy, the number-two man in the Bell organization. The dead man was Jim Walker, a recent addition to the Bell gang, but one of the men who had participated in the attempted robbery of the stagecoach. The names of the other men captured are not known.

A few weeks later, another informant got word to the sheriff in Camptonville that the debonair Monte Jack was hiding on the ranch of Jaime Ramirez. A small posse was formed, and when it charged the ranch house one member of the posse was critically wounded. A gunfight went on until dark, but when the lawmen cautiously entered the dwelling, they found only the body of Ramirez.

A short time later, the manager of the Oregon House, an inn in Yuba County, managed to get the drop on three more members of the Bell gang. He sent a patron for the sheriff and kept the frustrated outlaws immobilized at gunpoint for three hours until the sheriff arrived. Another member of the gang was picked up on the following day in Marysville, but still there was no sign of Tom Bell. A few days later, a breathless messenger informed Sheriff Henson of Placer County that Tom Bell and one of his men were eating in the Franklin House near Auburn.

When Henson and some of his deputies arrived at the Franklin House, two men, who had just mounted their horses, opened fire. In the ensuing gunfight, one of the outlaws was killed. The other got away. The dead man was Ned Connors, one of the charter members of the gang. The man who escaped was not Bell, but Bell had indeed been in the Franklin House, leaving about a half-hour before Henson appeared.

Detective Harrison, meanwhile, still had been spending a considerable amount of his time with the garrulous Brown, who was still being held in the Sacramento jail. During one of these discussions, Brown pulled out a bullet with a hole drilled through it and the attached string. When Harrison asked the meaning of the talisman, Brown told him it was a form of identification for the Bell gang. Then, almost as an afterthought, Brown told him of its use at the Western Exchange Hotel and of the continuing love affair between Elizabeth Hood and Tom Bell.

Harrison and Anderson once again picked up a couple of other lawmen and galloped off to the hotel on the Nevada City road. He was much too late. Elizabeth Hood had sold her interest in the hotel some ten days earlier and gone away with her three daughters. The present proprietor had no idea where she had gone, and even appeared to be surprised to learn that she was Tom Bell's girl.

He mentioned that she had left a letter in the saloon for a Bill White. Harrison went to the saloon. The letter had been picked up the previous day, but the bartender swore its recipient was not Tom Bell. "It could have been Bill Gristy, though," he added.

The letter had been left for Gristy. In it, Tom Bell told Gristy that it was time to lie low and move south. He had purchased a small ranch on the Stanislaus River near the forks of the Tuolume and the Merced. Elizabeth Hood and her daughters were there, along with two elderly brothers named Farnsworth, who were acting as caretakers for the property. If Gristy would meet him there, they could make plans for the future.

Gristy headed south after leaving the Western Exchange Hotel. He kept off the roads and successfully eluded the posses searching for him until he was several miles south of the area in which the Bell gang had operated. A few days later, he came to the town of Knight's Ferry. He was tired and hungry, and he decided he was so far south that it was unlikely anyone there had ever heard of Tom Bell. Having committed himself to this rationale, he rode boldly into town, tied up his horse in front of the Knight's Ferry Hotel, and entered the dining room.

Now Gristy's luck deserted him. The hotel was operated by T. W. Lane, a frequent visitor to San Francisco. Among his friends in that city was the warden of Angels Island Penitentiary, Jack Hayes. On one occasion, when Gristy had been in Hayes's custody, Lane had visited his friend and Hayes had pointed out Gristy as a notorious outlaw. On later visits to San Francisco, Lane had heard a great deal about Tom Bell and his chief lieutenant.

A surprised Lane acted with typical Western impulsiveness when he recognized the bandit seated at one of the dining-room tables. Lane walked behind the outlaw, put a gun to his head, and marched him to the Knight's Ferry jail. Gristy was not given enough time to sample the bowl of soup which the waiter placed before him.

It is not clear whether Gristy had Bell's letter in his possession when he was jailed. If he did, lawmen possibly learned of Bell's hideout from this. If not, Gristy was induced to tell his captors where his chief was hiding. As soon as this information was received, two citizens of Knight's Ferry were detailed to accompany Gristy to Marysville, where he would be turned over the the sheriff.

The law in Knight's Ferry was represented by an elderly town marshal who indicated that he had no desire to head up a posse to go after the notorious Tom Bell. Sheriff Joshua Malford and his two deputies were out looking for cattle rustlers, which was a point of some concern to Judge George Belt, who feared that Bell might flee. When two days passed with no sign of Sheriff Malford, Judge Belt decided to form a small vigilante group and go after Bell himself.

He had the directions to the hideout memorized. It was a small ranch near the swampy area around the Tulare Lakes about six miles above Firebaugh's Ferry. Belt and his vigilantes arrived at the ranch on September 28, a Sunday. Elizabeth Hood and her three young daughters were in the residence. The Farnsworth brothers were napping in a small cottage in back of the larger ranch house. The vigilantes told the Farnsworths to disappear, gave Elizabeth an hour to gather up her personal possessions, then detached one member of the group to drive her and her daughters in a buckboard to Stockton, where, she said, she had friends. The vigilantes then settled down to wait for Tom Bell to return to his mistress.

On Monday afternoon, a posse headed by Sheriff Malford arrived at the ranch. Malford had run across Gristy and his two guards as they proceeded toward Marysville, and Gristy had given him the same information given to the town marshal and Judge Belt in Knight's Ferry. There still was no sign of Bell. On the following Friday, Sheriff Malford decided that the wait was not only tiresome but nonsensical as well. It was obvious that Tom Bell had been told of the trap. Early Friday afternoon, Malford gathered up his posse and headed down the river to Stockton. Judge Belt and his vigilantes decided to wait one more day, but by Saturday noon he had reached the same conclusion as had Malford. The vigilantes packed up.

One of the vigilantes was a man named Robert Price. He had put off a business trip to Sonora to join the vigilante group. Now that these men were returning to Knight's Ferry, Price decided to go directly to Sonora from the ranch. As a result, he bid farewell to his friends and struck off in a northerly direction. He forded a small stream and came out behind a small grove of willows. A movement caught his eye, and he paused. Hiding in the willows was a solitary man on a horse intently watching the slow exodus of Judge Belt and his fellow citizens. Quietly, Price moved away from the grove.

He crossed the stream about a mile down the river, intercepted Judge Belt, and told him what he had seen. The judge and one other man accompanied Price back to the willow grove. The man was still there, resting quietly on his horse and watching the cabin. He did not hear the trio until the men were almost on top of him; then he grabbed quickly at the rifle in its scabbard. He paused as Judge Belt raised his double-barreled shotgun.

"I believe," said Judge Belt, "that you are the man we have been looking for."

"Very probably," the man replied.

"Are you Tom Bell?" The question was unnecessary. The disfigured nose told that it was the bandit.

Bell was taken from his horse and, with his arms bound to his sides, led at the end of a rope to Firebaugh's Ferry. At the edge of the town was an empty cabin near a large sycamore tree. "This will do," Judge Belt said. "Would you like a shot of whiskey?"

The outlaw shook his head. "I would like to write a couple of letters."

"Of course," Judge Belt replied.

The letters were addressed to Elizabeth Hood and to his mother, in Nashville, and both were published later in the San Francisco *Alta*.

> Firebaugh's Ferry, Oct. 4, 1856
> Mrs. Hood, my dear and only friend now in this country:
> As I am not allowed the liberty of seeing you, I have been given the privilege of writing you a few lines as I have but a few moments to live. I am at a great loss for something to say. I have been most foully betrayed. Bill and John have told things that never took place. I am accused of every robbery that has been committed for the past twelve months, which is entirely false. I have never committed but three highway robberies in my life, but still I am to blame and my fate is sealed. I am to die like a dog and there is but one thing that grieves me and that is the condition of you and your family. Probably I have been the instrumentality of your misfortunes. In my last moments, I will think of the many favors you have done for me and if I had fifty kingdoms to

present you should have them all. But alas! I am poor and my fate is sealed. I would like to give you some advice but I fear you may think me presumptuous. What I would like to say is this: That you had better send the girls to San Francisco to the Sisters of Charity. There they will be educated and taken care of. Tell all the girls farewell. Tell them to be good girls and to be very careful to whom they pledge themselves for life. All the money I have is ten dollars which I have given to Mr. Chism for Sarah. If you ever see Edward, tell him my fate. I must come to a close for the hounds are thirsting for my blood. Good-bye forever.

Thos. J. Bell

Time was getting short, and the letter to his mother was briefer.

Dear Mother:

As I am about to make my exit to another country, I take this opportunity to write you a few lines. Probably you may never hear from me again. If not, I hope we may meet where parting is no more.

In my prodigal career in this country, I have always recollected your fond admonitions and, if I had lived up to them probably I would not have been in my present condition; but dear Mother, though my fate has been a cruel one, yet I have no one to blame but myself. Give my respects to all of old and youthful friends. Tell them to beware of bad associations and never to enter into any gambling saloons, for that has been my ruin.

I bid you farewell forever.

Your only boy,
Tom

It now was four o'clock in the afternoon, The vigilantes were becoming impatient. The three men who stood over him while he wrote his letters prodded him, and he stood up. With a vigilante on each side of him, Tom Bell was led out of the cabin to the sycamore tree, where a hangman's rope had been thrown over one branch. As the noose was adjusted around his neck, Bell commented almost casually, "You know, I am twenty-six years old." Seconds later, the vigilantes pulled on the other end of the rope, hoisting Tom Bell into the air and slowly strangling him to death.

Word of Tom Bell's hanging was slow in getting out, probably because of the lynching. Some of the papers in the Mother Lode country, such as the San Andreas *Independent,* reported the hanging. Other newspapers, such as the *Alta,* speculated that Tom Bell had circulated the rumor as a cover for his escape. More than a month after his death, a rumor spread around Gold Flat in the northern Mother Lode country that Tom Bell was hiding in an isolated mountain cabin. A posse set out to capture him. When the horsemen neared the cabin, they split into two groups. One group approached the cabin from the rear, the other from the front. Each group thought it had flushed the bandits, and they began firing at each other. When the melee finally settled, four men were dead and three others critically wounded. There was no one in the cabin.

As with Murietta, the story still persists that Tom Bell escaped, that he went back to Nashville and practiced medicine or slipped into Mexico. It is possible. There is no record of his grave or of the disposition of his body. But whether he was hanged by the vigilantes in Firebaugh's Ferry or lived to a comfortable old age, Tom Hodges, alias Tom Bell, marked the beginning of an era in Western banditry. He was the first man to attempt to rob a stagecoach, but there were hundreds of outlaws who preyed on this lumbering vehicle during the next sixty years.

The last of the stagecoach robberies was so successful that the loot has never been found, and it attracted very little attention. It occurred just outside the isolated town of Jarbidge, Nevada, near the Idaho border.

To reach the remains of Jarbidge today requires considerable driving skill. The narrow road twists and slideslips almost twenty-five hundred feet down the side of a canyon in a distance of less than five miles. The road was even more hazardous in 1916, when Jarbidge was only eight years old. The grade was steeper and the road much more narrow. One reporter who made the trip into the community by stagecoach described the trail as less than a foot wider than the conveyance, adding that at certain places there was not room to allow a man on horseback to pass.

At least two stage drivers are known to have lost their lives on the hazardous road. One was killed when an avalanche pushed the stage into a deep ravine. The other died when the horses bolted off the road during a heavy blizzard.

The road was the only link between Jarbidge and Rogerson, Idaho, approximately sixty-five miles to the north. The stagecoach scheduled three trips a week into the remote mining town, usually arriving at about three in the afternoon. On December 5, 1916, the stage was late. This was not considered unusual. There had been several snow flurries earlier in the day, and there also had been reports of an avalanche near the Dixie Mine. The road was icy and slippery, and the driver could be expected to exercise care.

There is some disagreement over the name of the stagecoach driver on that day. Some accounts identify him as F. M. Searcy. Another reports his name as Frank Slattery, but, whatever his name, he was a doomed man.

When night fell and the stage still had not arrived, the postmaster in Jarbidge sent a couple of men on horseback to search for it. They returned several hours later to report that they had ridden to the top of the pass and had seen no signs of it, nor were there any visible signs that it had skidded off the road into the canyon. The postmaster and practically everyone else in Jarbidge assumed that either the stage had not left Rogerson or it had broken down somewhere on the pass. The delay would have an effect on nearly everyone in the town. In the stage strongbox was more than forty thousand dollars in cash, of which thirty thousand dollars was the payroll for the employees of four mines. The remaining ten thousand dollars was being shipped to the Jarbidge bank and the town's local gambling saloon.

Shortly after noon on the following day, a freight wagon from Rogerson arrived in Jarbidge. The two teamsters reported that the stage had left Idaho on schedule the preceding day. They had followed the same route that stages ordinarily took, but had seen no signs of it.

A more intensive search was launched. It was the consensus that the stage had slipped off the road and that the skid marks had been erased by the winds and snow flurries. The searchers went several miles past the summit, but no trace of the missing stage could be found.

Shortly before dusk, Mrs. Dexter, an elderly widow who lived about two miles north of the center of town, appeared in the general store and post office to pick up her mail. When told that the stagecoach apparently had gone off the grade, Mrs. Dexter shook her head. "Nonsense," she replied. "It passed my house about five o'clock last night."

Mrs. Dexter was known to be a little confused at times, but she insisted that on the previous night she had seen the stage pass her house. "It was snowing, and the driver was all slouched down into his greatcoat," she insisted. "If I could have caught him I would have asked him in for a cup of warm tea."

The postmaster was still skeptical, but he dispatched a couple of men to canvass the area between the town and Mrs. Dexter's modest cottage. The searchers found the stagecoach in a small grove of trees about three hundred yards off the highway and less than a mile from the center of town. The horses, nearly dead from the cold, were still in harness. The search party could not move the coach, for the brakes were frozen to the wheel rims. Frozen to an inside seat in the coach by his own blood was the driver. There were bullet holes in both his head and chest. The strongbox, on the ground, was empty, its lock shot away. The money was missing.

The postmaster was the town marshal, and he launched an investigation of the crime the next morning, helped by several shocked citizens. He decided there were two spots where the ambush of the stage might have occurred. One was about a mile north of the Dexter cottage, where tracks in the road indicated that the stagecoach had slithered from one side to the other for a distance of about seventy-five yards. If that was where the driver had been shot, it meant that the murderer had been driving the stage when it was seen by Mrs. Dexter. The other possible ambush site was at a point about fifty yards north of the grove of trees where the stage had been hidden. Bloodstains were found there under some freshly fallen snow.

A small creek ran along the side of the grove farthest from the road. A path had been trod into the ground beside the stream, over which a flimsy footbridge had been built to provide a shortcut into town for Mrs. Dexter and the few other persons who lived on that side of the community. No one could be found who had heard any gunfire, but along the path and on the bridge the postmaster and his amateur sleuths made what they thought was a significant discovery: the prints of a man and a dog.

One of the miners who lived in Jarbidge was a young man named Benjamin Kuhl. He was of surly disposition, and the only friend he had in the community was his dog, a large yellow mongrel. The dog was as friendly as his master was unfriendly, and it was no chore for the postmaster to entice the animal away from Kuhl's cabin and take him out to the grove. The pawprints in the snow matched those of the dog, according to testimony offered later.

The dog, however, pointed a paw of suspicion toward his master in a much more dramatic manner. After his pawprint had been compared, the animal bounded over to a fallen log and began barking and digging at its side. The investigators raised the log. Underneath it were a bloodstained shirt and coat. The shirt, a black-and-white woolen check, was similar to one worn by Kuhl. One of the citizens identified the coat as Kuhl's property.

The postmaster led his team back to Kuhl's cabin. There, under the bed, they found a revolver with three shots fired from it. The records do not indicate whether the weapon was the same caliber as that of the gun used in the murder of the stagecoach driver. There was no sign of the loot.

When Kuhl returned to his cabin, he was arrested by his fellow townsmen and driven in a buckboard to distant Elko, where he was turned over to the sheriff to await trial. He denied any knowledge of the crime and claimed the gun was not his. He denied ever owning a gun. He produced witnesses at his trial who stated that Kuhl had been in a Jarbidge saloon on the evening of the murder. On cross-examination, however, the witnesses were not sure which night they had seen Kuhl.

The defendant's lawyer pointed out that Kuhl quite probably would have been stricken with pneumonia had he walked bare-chested to his cabin from the spot where he allegedly had buried his coat and shirt. The jury did not accept this logic, however. It found Kuhl guilty of first-degree murder and, according to custom, recommended that he be hanged. The sentence was commuted by the judge, however, to life imprisonment. Kuhl served twenty-seven years in the Nevada State Prison in Carson City. He was released in 1944. Three days after his release, Kuhl was killed by a hit-and-run driver as he walked along the highway between Elko and Jarbidge.

It was the end of an era in the American West, an era launched by Tom Bell some sixty years earlier. Kuhl was the last man to hold up a stagecoach.

That hijacker took the ultimate risk. He showed
real drama, mystery, heroic features, romanticism, skill and
all the necessities of a perfect crime. His motive was simple—
$200,000, and people understand that much better.

D. B. Cooper

THE legend sur-
rounding D. B. Cooper is in its formative stage. Two popular songs
have been recorded which glorify the man known as D. B. Cooper.
Young men and women and boys and girls wear T-shirts which
portray an artist's conception of this mysterious man and ask plain-

tively, D. B. COOPER, WHERE ARE YOU? Bumper stickers on cars ask the same question.

The man they refer to actually never called himself D. B. Cooper. This modern bandit, who struck once and escaped with two hundred thousand dollars, used the alias Dan Cooper. In the uproar that occurred during the bandit's spectacular coup, someone said he had identified himself as D. B. Cooper, and it is this name that is making the legend. It really doesn't make much difference. Neither was the real name of this methodical bandit. No one has the slightest clue as to his real identity. He first attracted public attention on the afternoon of November 24, 1971, when he became the first man in history to hijack a plane for ransom.

Northwest Orient Airlines Flight 305 took a long time to cross the country. It originated in Washington, D.C., and its final destination was Seattle, Washington. It made many stops between the two cities: Minneapolis, Minnesota; Great Falls and Missoula in Montana; Spokane, Washington; Portland, Oregon; and finally Seattle.

On November 24, 1971, the day before Thanksgiving, it left the nation's capital at eight thirty A.M., and it adhered reasonably well to its schedule until it departed Portland for its usual half-hour flight to Seattle.

The aircraft was a Boeing 727-100 jet. The forward entrance required either a jetway or stairs. The rear entrance utilized stairs that were built into the aircraft. These ventral steps were located in the rear center of the plane, and could be lowered and raised by punching a button on the adjacent bulkhead.

Although it was a mid-afternoon before a festive holiday, the passenger load on Flight 305 was light. Only a dozen persons waited to board the plane at Portland for the final leg of its journey. One of these passengers was a man in his mid-thirties who, despite the rain and overcast outside, affected a pair of dark glasses. He did nothing to attract attention to himself. One of the airline employees described him later as "bulky," with thinning hair. He wore a dark, conservative business suit and dark brown oxford shoes. He arrived at the Northwest ticket counter about forty-five minutes before Flight 305 landed, and there he purchased a one-way ticket for cash to Seattle, telling the agent his name was Dan Cooper.

He carried an attaché case and a brown paper bag of medium size. Light baggage was not unusual for passengers flying between Portland and Seattle. There was a considerable amount of commuter traffic between those two cities, and passengers often went back and forth in one day.

Several minutes before the flight was called, "Cooper" went to the gate and waited patiently in order that he might be the first of the Portland passengers to board the jet. After he entered the aircraft, he chose a seat in the last row of the plane.

The plane taxied out to the runway and took off routinely. As soon as the "no-smoking" light had been extinguished, he pressed the stewardess call button. Stewardess Florence Schaffner answered the summons. He smiled thinly and passed her a small folded piece of paper. Florence Schaffner still carried her purse from a strap slung over her shoulder. "I thought he was trying to hustle me," she said later. "I stuffed the piece of paper in my purse, but he angrily motioned for me to take it out and read it."

Richard Simmons, a passenger sitting across the aisle watched the byplay between the flight attendant and the man. "I saw the stewardess answer the call," he said. When she read the note, "her face dropped. She looked bewildered. I guess she knew what was happening then."

Florence Schaffner indeed knew what was happening. The note was terse. Upon the arrival of the aircraft in Seattle, the sum of two hundred thousand dollars and four parachutes were to be brought on board the plane. Then, as she looked once again toward the passenger, he picked up the attaché case, placed it in his lap, and raised the lid. Inside the case were two large cylinders and a tangle of wires.

She was looking at a powerful bomb, he said, and unless his instructions were followed to the letter, he would blow up the airplane. There was nothing remarkable about his voice. His diction was good, and she could place no regional accent. Florence Schaffner nodded, spun around, and carried the note forward to the pilot, Captain William W. Scott. He read the note and listened to the stewardess's description of the contents of the attaché case.

There had been several aircraft hijackings in the United States within the immediately preceding years, but most had been politically motivated, or carried out by mentally deranged persons. The objective of these hijackings was to get free transportation to Cuba or Africa, places, it was hoped, of political asylum. Other hijackers were robbers or rapists seeking escape, but this was the first time a bandit had attempted to holdup an airline for profit: an aerial highwayman.

Picking up his microphone, Captain Scott radioed the details of the situation on board the aircraft to Seattle ground control and to the carrier's operations office. He then sent the stewardess back to the hijacker with the word that he would follow the bandit's instructions.

Florence Schaffner returned. The first order from the bandit was to circle over the mountains until the money and the parachutes were brought to the airport. Scott followed the instructions to the letter.

It was mid-afternoon when the man to be known as D. B. Cooper took over the aircraft. It was shortly before five P.M. in Minneapolis, Minnesota, where Northwest Orient Airlines maintains its general offices, and the airline's president, Donald W. Nyrop, was still in his office. He issued orders to cooperate fully with the hijacker. "Do whatever he demands," Nyrop said.

The hijacker was demanding two hundred thousand dollars. A series of telephone calls was made from the airline's headquarters in Minneapolis to banks in the Seattle area. Airline officials scurried to these banks, and in less than an hour after the aircraft had been commandeered, the two hundred thousand dollars had been gathered, in twenty-dollar bills. Meanwhile, the Federal Bureau of Investigation had been notified, as had other local police officials. The captured plane circled over nearby Mount Rainier as the serial numbers of the bills were noted by the F.B.I. Newsmen gathered at Seatac Airport.

It took longer to get the four parachutes than it did the money. The only parachute that could be found at the Seattle airport was a model that was used for training and was inoperable. A sports-type chute was found in nearby Renton. A request for four chutes was made to the Air Force at McChord Air Force Base, but, in a typical military snafu, only two were sent to Seatac Airport. At about five fifteen P.M., Pacific time, word was sent to Scott that the parachutes and the money were waiting for the bandit.

Florence Schaffner relayed the information from Scott to the bandit. "Go ahead and land," Cooper said.

The pilot headed for the airport, apologizing to the other passengers for the delay.

Flight 305 landed in Seattle at five forty P.M. It did not go to the terminal building. It was directed to a more remote section of the airport. No one immediately approached the aircraft. Scott had warned everyone to stay away "until we get coordinated with our friend in the back."

It took a little while to get coordinated, and accounts are sketchy as to what occurred during the first moments after the plane rolled to a stop. Barbara Simmons, another passenger who sat near the bandit, recalled, "It was all rather strange when the plane landed. We sat there for a quarter of an hour. No one talked. No one moved."

Then one of the stewardesses came down the aisle and pushed the button that lowered the rear stairs. The bandit slowly rose from his seat and picked up an intercom telephone by the top of the rear stairs. Again there was a long wait. Then an airline official came to the bottom of the stairs. He carried the parachutes up two at a time, then came back with the money in a satchel-type bag. The bandit threw them all onto the seats in the last row. He opened the satchel and looked briefly at the money, but did not count it. He then spoke again into the intercom.

The captain's voice followed immediately over the public-address system. "All passengers may disembark through the rear entrance," Scott said.

The passengers lined up and went down the stairs. Most of them kept their eyes down as they passed the bandit, who now was back in his seat, holding his attaché case. He still wore his dark glasses.

Florence Schaffner and another stewardess followed the passengers down the stairs. The third stewardess, Tina Mucklow, walked down the aisle toward the exit, but the bandit stopped her. "You will stay on board," he said. Tina Mucklow went back to the flight deck.

Again there was a long wait. Then the bandit buzzed the cockpit area on the intercom. "Let's go to Mexico," he said. He spoke as if he was suggesting a party.

Captain Scott told him that Mexico was beyond the range of the aircraft.

"Not if we refuel in Reno."

"I'll try to make the necessary arrangements." The captain relayed the latest demands to the tower and his operations center. Again there was a long wait.

An official of the Federal Aviation Authority started up the rear stairs. The bandit sensed the movement and abruptly ordered the government official off the plane. Then he spoke to Scott, and his voice was menacing. "Let's get this show on the road," he snapped.

Scott picked up his microphone. "This guy is getting antsy," he reported.

Another quarter-hour passed. Then Scott was told that Northwest Airlines had made arrangements to have the aircraft refueled in Reno, Nevada. Scott sent Tina Mucklow back with the message.

The bandit smiled. His irritation had passed. "Then please close the door and let's go," he said.

The stewardess paused after the steps were raised and the door was closed.

"Go and join the crew on the flight deck," the bandit ordered. She went forward.

As the three-engine jet slowly taxied toward the runway, the bandit once again buzzed the captain on the intercom. He was explicit in his directions. The ship would fly the straightest possible course to Reno, Nevada, The ground speed would be precisely two hundred miles per hour. His altitude at cruising would be ten thousand feet, and he would fly with the flaps extended to fifteen degrees. Scott suddenly knew the bandit was a pilot and that he was familiar with the flight characteristics of the Boeing 727.

There was a long delay at the takeoff runway. This delay was deliberate, for it was to allow time for two F-106 fighters from McChord Air Force Base to become airborne and follow the captured 727. After about ten minutes, the bandit once again called. "What now?" he asked.

"Traffic control."

The bandit accepted the excuse, lending further credence to the theory that he was an experienced pilot. Almost another quarter-hour passed before the military jets radioed that they were in position to follow.

The two pursuing jet fighters picked up the 727 as it made its climb out of Seatac Airport. The chase turned out to be an extraordinarily difficult one. The F-106 could not fly at such a slow speed safely, but both pilots mushed their planes approximately five miles behind the 727.

At ten thousand feet, Scott leveled the jet. A moment later, the intercom buzzed for the last time. "Send the stewardess back with my note," the bandit said.

Tina Mucklow carried the note back to the hijacker. He still sat in the last row of seats, his hands on the attaché case. As she passed him the note, she saw that he had taken the cover from one of the parachutes and had filled it with the twenty-dollar bills. The bandit took the note from the girl, thanked her courteously, and told her to return to the flight deck. That was the last time any of the crew ever saw their mysterious passenger.

Meanwhile, back at Seatac Airport, FBI agents finished their interrogation of the thirty-five passengers and two stewardesses who had disembarked from Flight 305. Checking the names against the manifest, they learned that the man still on board the aircraft had given the name of Dan Cooper when he purchased his ticket. Because it was a cash sale and the departure of the aircraft was imminent when the sale was consummated, there had been no attempt to secure a home address or telephone contact. A reporter asked one of the deputy sheriffs for the name of the missing passenger.

"Cooper."

"First name?"

The deputy shook his head. "There were just initials, D. B." he replied.

Thus, D. B. Cooper, whose name was to become legendary, was born. The news wire services carried it around the world as D. B. Cooper, and that is the name by which he is known today.

In the Boeing 727, Scott turned the aircraft on a direct heading for Reno, Nevada. The plane was running on reserve fuel, and if he had to seek an alternate airport to Reno, he could be in trouble. Clouds covered the ground below, and there was some turbulence. A red light came on over his head: The rear stairs of the jet were being lowered. A few seconds later, he felt the aircraft slow slightly as the projected stairs increased the plane's drag. He looked at his watch and his map. He was twenty minutes away from Seattle, and, at that speed, about thirty-five miles northeast of Portland. A moment later it became very cold inside the plane as the heat was sucked out through the open door. Oddly, although Scott made a notation of his position when the stairs were lowered, neither he nor any of the other members of the crew thought the bandit had bailed out. It was not a good spot to jump. Parts of the terrain were open, cultivated fields, but other parts were dense forest, and there were rivers and lakes which could prove hazardous to a night jumper. He continued toward Reno.

No one talked much in the cockpit. It was too cold. Two hours and twenty minutes later, the plane flared out for a landing at the Reno airport. The bottom of the stairs struck the runway, and the locks on the stairwell snapped in a shower of sparks as the plane settled down. When the plane came to a stop at the end of the runway, Tina Mucklow once again left the cockpit and went back into the rear cabin. The bandit had disappeared. Gone also were his attaché case, his paper bag, and two of the parachutes. The cover of a third chute had been removed, and the chute was "popped." The satchel in which the money had been carried to the plane was missing, as was the third chute cover, and, of course, the two hundred thousand dollars.

There are conflicting reports as to which two parachutes the bandit had taken for his jump. One report states that the inoperable training chute was gone. Another states that this had been left behind on the plane.

The military jet pilots had seen nothing.

It now was presumed that the bandit had jumped shortly after the rear door had been opened. This theory was substantiated a short time later when an analysis of the aircraft's flight recorder indicated a slight change in the flying altitude of the plane at that time.

A posse was formed. Thirty sheriff deputies from Cowlitz and Clark Counties in southwestern Washington were joined by an army of FBI agents. Using Scott's notes and the information gleaned from the flight recorder, it was decided that the bandit had left the aircraft somewhere between the small towns of Aerial and Amboy. The winds in the area were reported to have been gusty and heavy at the time, so the original search by the posse on Thanksgiving morning covered a much larger area. It included a grid ten miles wide and fifteen miles long between Aerial and the city of Longview, Washington, on the banks of the Columbia River. The area was, as Scott remembered it, dense with trees in some parts, open with clearings in others. Outside the grid, but nearby, was the artificial Lake Merwin, a cold and deep body of water dammed up in a canyon.

The weather was still bad. Low clouds massed over the area, closing off the possibility of a helicopter search. For two days, this posse of police experts combed the area, but the searchers were left scratching their heads. There was not the slightest sign of the bandit, D. B. Cooper, or the two hundred thousand dollars.

As the search continued into the weekend, the posse fanned out. It was a rural area. The houses were far apart. One member of the posse stopped to visit with a farmer near Aerial named Donald Haun. Adjacent to his farm was a seldom-used landing strip that had been there since before the Hauns had acquired the property, some years earlier.

On the night preceding the holdup of Flight 305, Haun and his wife heard a small airplane land on the strip. Looking out the window, they saw that the strip had been illuminated by the lights of a car. The plane remained on the ground but a few minutes. After it took off, the car remained. The plane returned about forty-five minutes later, landed, and took off again immediately. This time the car also left. They did not know if the incident was repeated on the night of the holdup: The Hauns had attended a wedding in Amboy. Amele Neiger and his wife, Anna, also heard a plane flying low the night before the holdup. They had attended the same wedding on Thanksgiving Eve, as had every one else in the vicinity.

Another odd thing happened that night, however, in that area about thirty-five miles northeast of Portland. Just Hatfield heard a heavy thump on his roof and something fall and scrape. He picked up his rifle, loaded it, and went outside. He could find nothing.

Mrs. Melvin Anderson, who lived some distance from the Haun farm, recalled hearing a small plane on both nights, but did not hear it land. She made no attempt to see it on either night.

On Sunday, the sullen clouds rolled back to the Pacific, and military helicopters were brought in. They coursed over a huge area, looking for an abandoned parachute. They found nothing. A couple of days later, winter arrived and snow covered the higher elevations. The posse abandoned the search.

Northwest Airlines posted a twenty-five-thousand-dollar reward for information leading to the arrest of D. B. Cooper and the return of the ransom. The Oregon *Journal* in Portland offered a thousand-dollar check to anyone who brought in the first twenty-dollar bill with a serial number which matched one of those taken by D. B. Cooper. A man named D. B. Cooper in Spokane, Washington, was forced to have his telephone unlisted. Too many persons thought it a hilarious joke to call him up and ask to share the loot. Some of the calls were made from as far away as Portland and Seattle.

In the spring, the military launched an "Operation Recover." For days helicopters skimmed along the ground at treetop level. Troops canvassed an area thirty miles square. Residents of the area were unimpressed. Cows ran themselves to death. Horses disappeared. A body—that of a murder victim—was discovered. There was no trace of D. B. Cooper. On the day the search was abandoned, another body—this time a woman's—was found, and another missing-persons case was erased from the books.

When the military left, the treasure seekers came. They came in droves from as far away as Los Angeles and Chicago. There had been many reports that D. B. Cooper could not possibly have survived a parachute jump in the bad weather that prevailed at the time, that his body, with two hundred thousand dollars strapped to it, was surely snagged on the heavy branch of a Douglas fir tree. The treasure seekers didn't frighten cattle, and they spent money. They were welcomed by the community.

Songstress Joan Savage recorded the first song of the exploits of D. B. Cooper, who had ripped off the Establishment with such finesse. Bumper stickers appeared on cars: D. B. COOPER, WHERE ARE YOU? A D. B. Cooper fan club was organized in Portland, and D. B. Cooper T-shirts became popular.

Despite the publicity accorded him by his fans and the activities of the treasure seekers, D. B. Cooper remained as elusive and mysterious as ever. He had become a hero.

"We all like adventure stories," Dr. Otto Larsen, sociology professor at the University of Washington, told a national news magazine. "That hijacker took the greatest ultimate risk. He showed real heroic features: mystery, drama, romanticism, skill, and all the necessities for a perfect crime. His motive was simply two hundred thousand dollars, and people can understand that much better."

There were others who tried to emulate D. B. Cooper. A police officer from Provo, Utah, ransomed a United Airlines 727 for three thousand dollars and bailed out successfully near his home. Before putting his plan into action, however, he had discussed it with a relative, who pointed police in his direction. The ransom was recovered from an underground cache in his back yard. Another attempt was made aboard an Eastern Airlines plane. This time one million dollars was collected. The money was first delivered in small bills, then sent back with a request that it be resubmitted in thousand- and five-hundred-dollar bills. When this was done, the hijacker was flown to Honduras, where he bailed out. He was quickly caught by Honduran authorities, who returned him to the United States.

The Boeing 727 and the McDonnell Douglas DC-9 were the only commercial jet aircraft with the ventral stairwell in the rear of the plane. Frustrated and angry airline officials met to discuss ways of blocking this new wave of hijackings. Before they could come up with a solution, a Southern Airways DC-9 was held up for two million dollars. This hijacker did not attempt to parachute. He forced the pilot to fly to Havana, Cuba. The money was confiscated by the Cuban Government and later returned to the carrier. The hijacker was jailed.

The manufacturers of the aircraft came up with a device which was to block parachuting bandits. It was a small electronic lock that prevented anyone from activating the ventral stairwell while the plane was in flight. It worked. No parachuting bandit has held up an airline since these devices were installed. Thus, D. B. Cooper apparently was the only successful plane robber.

Or was he successful? The debate still goes on. The FBI still carries it as an open case. Gene Cotton, who was sheriff of Clark County when D. B. Cooper came into being, thought the bandit was thoroughly successful in his holdup. "With the FBI and the army searching for him, he would have been found if he was still in there," Cotton said.

No one answering his description ever was reported missing. Such a report probably would be made if he were suspended somewhere from the branch of a Douglas fir.

Leverett Richards, the knowledgeable aviation editor of the *Oregonian,* disagreed with Cotton. "It is very improbable that he could have survived the jump. The weather was extremely bad that night, cold and freezing. Even at the two-hundred-miles-per-hour speed the plane was traveling that night, the shock of the wind would have ripped off his shoes. He probably went into Lake Merwin and is on the bottom, weighted down by his parachutes and his loot."

On the other hand, two other skyjackers easily bailed out of a commercial jet liner through the ventral stairwell. What had D. B. Cooper carried in his brown paper sack? Could it have been a change of clothing, a pair of paraboots? What happened to the satchel, the attaché case? He would have kicked those out of the open door rather than carry them in his jump.

Still, planes have gone down in the dense forests of the Pacific Northwest and not been found for years. And what about the two hundred thousand dollars? Not one of the ten thousand twenty-dollar bills has ever shown up, yet every bank in the nation was alerted to the serial numbers of the bills given to D. B. Cooper.

Northwest Orient Airlines sued its insurance company for

restitution of the money it paid to the bandit, and in 1975 the courts ruled that the insurance company would have to pay the money to the carrier.

As soon as the money was paid, the airline withdrew its twenty-five-thousand-dollar reward for the capture of D. B. Cooper.

Every summer the treasure seekers appear around Aerial and Amboy. Some wear T-shirts that ask, D. B. COOPER, WHERE ARE YOU?

The legend goes on.